CANADA A PORTRAIT

© Minister of Industry, 1999

Available in Canada through authorized bookstore agents and other bookstores or from:

Statistics Canada
Circulation Management
Dissemination Division
120 Parkdale Avenue
Ottawa, Ontario
K1A 0T6
Toll Free Order Line: 1 800 267-6677
Fax: 1 877 287-4369
E-mail: order@statcan.ca

Design: Neville Smith, Aviva Furman
Composition: Dissemination Division

Printed by Friesens Corporation
Altona, Manitoba

The National Library of Canada has catalogued this publication as follows:

Main entry under title:

Canada: A Portrait

56th ed.
"The official handbook of present conditions and recent progress."
Issued also in French under title: Un portrait du Canada,
Continues: Canada handbook, the . . . handbook of present conditions and recent progress.

Catalogue No. 11-403-XPE
ISBN 0-660-17780-3

1. Canada – Economic conditions - Periodicals.
2. Canada – Social conditions – Periodicals.
3. Canada – Politics and government - Periodicals.
4. Canada – Description and travel - Periodicals.
5. Canada – Handbooks, manuals, etc. 1. Statistics Canada. Communications Division.

La présente publication est également disponible en français.

Printed in Canada

THE OFFICIAL MILLENNIAL

AND 56TH EDITION OF

CANADA: A PORTRAIT,

PUBLISHED UNDER THE

AUTHORITY OF THE

MINISTER OF INDUSTRY

FOREWORD

CANADA STANDS AT A UNIQUE POINT IN TIME AND PLACE, AS WE ENTER THE 21ST CENTURY AND A NEW MILLENNIUM. TO NOTE THIS SPECIAL MOMENT, I AM PROUD TO PRESENT THIS DISTINCTIVE EDITION OF *CANADA: A PORTRAIT* AS STATISTICS CANADA'S CONTRIBUTION TO OUR NATIONAL CELEBRATIONS.

SINCE IT FIRST APPEARED IN 1927, *CANADA: A PORTRAIT* HAS CHRONICLED THE SOCIAL, ECONOMIC AND INTELLECTUAL LIFE OF THIS COUNTRY. THIS 56TH EDITION BUILDS ON THIS TRADITION, OFFERING READERS AN EXPANDED COLLECTION OF ESSAYS AND PHOTOGRAPHS WHICH FRAME AND ILLUMINATE OUR STATISTICAL WORK.

I AM ESPECIALLY HONOURED TO SIGNAL THE CONTRIBUTIONS OF SIX ACCOMPLISHED CANADIANS WHO HAVE ADDED THEIR OWN "PORTRAITS" OF CANADA. MANY THANKS TO SUSAN AGLUKARK, PIERRE BERTON, RICHARD LIPSEY, MONIQUE MERCURE, OSCAR PETERSON AND DAVID SUZUKI.

CANADA: A PORTRAIT CONTINUES TO BREAK NEW GROUND IN THE WAY WE PRESENT STATISTICS TO THE PUBLIC. IT IS MY SINCERE HOPE THAT IT WILL OFFER A CLEAR VIEW OF CANADA TODAY, AND THUS INFORM AND REMIND FUTURE GENERATIONS OF WHERE WE WERE AT THE START OF THIS NEW CENTURY AND MILLENNIUM. I AM PLEASED TO RECOMMEND IT TO ALL OUR READERS.

Ivan P. Fellegi
Chief Statistician of Canada

THE TEAM

On behalf of Statistics Canada, I wish to acknowledge and thank all those who have worked on this millennial edition of *Canada: A Portrait*. As the 2000 *Portrait* continues its tradition of combining the creative and the analytic in telling its story of the people of Canada, it has been enriched and strengthened by all who have worked on it.

Together with Janet Hagey, Director of Communications, I am honoured to signal the contributions of the *Portrait* team.

Under the very skillful guidance of Laurel Hyatt, Production Manager and Senior Editor, a team of writers and editors came together, bringing a fresh and vital approach to the text. We thank Julie Bélanger, Pat Buchanan, Alan Bulley, Kevin Burns, Valérie Catrice, Gilbert Côté, Judith Côté, Mélanie Desjardins, Christine Duchesne, Francine Dumas, Monique Dumont, Mark Foss, Sherry Galey, Alain Garneau, Jocelyn Harvey, Susan Hickman, Elizabeth Irving, Bruce Nesbitt, Geoff Poapst, Gordon Priest, Penny Stuart, Marie-Pierre Tarte, Nathalie Turcotte and Nathalie Villemure.

Much appreciation also to Janis Camelon as mentor of the English editors, and to Annie Lebeau for direction of the French editing team. Thanks also to Jeannot Trudel for astute translations and to Marie-Anne Bradford, Sylvette Cadieux and Martin Blais for their timeliness and guidance with all our translation requests.

Special appreciation must go to Maxine Davidson, who as Production Co-ordinator brought order to our publishing life, and to Brigitte Angrignon, her assistant. Many thanks also to Nick Thorp for assiduous fact-checking, to Caroline Tremblay for assistance, and to Andrew Neish for friendly support.

For analytic skills, we are indebted to experts within Statistics Canada: Paul Blouin, Mary Cromie, Tim Davis, Chris Jackson, Andrew Kohut, Rebecca Kong, Lucie Laliberté, Janice McMechan, Paul McPhie, Hans Messinger, Steven Mozes, François Nault, Shaila Nijhowne, Henry Puderer, Paul Reed, Art Ridgeway, Krishna Sahay, Jim Seidle, Pierre Turcotte, John Turner, Stu Wells, Karen Wilson and Paula Woollam.

We are grateful also to Professor John Warkentin of York University and to Jacques Lefebvre for mentoring *Portrait* writers and staff.

Special appreciation to Johanne Beauseigle for competent and shrewd technical management, and especially to Louise Demers, head of composition, and her team, Suzanne Beauchamp and Lynne Durocher, who worked tirelessly to bring the book to life. We are also grateful to Danielle Baum for skilled technical expertise. Our thanks and appreciation to Jacques Tessier who successfully shepherded the project through the printing world.

Our gratitude also to Wayne Baxter, Mary Rigby and Gabrielle Beaudoin for marketing strategies and to Iain McKellar and John Whitton for innovations on the sales front.

We wish to extend heartfelt appreciation to the staff of Statistics Canada's library, who have offered us continued support and insightful guidance.

We are honoured to have worked with Neville Smith and Aviva Furman, whose designs have brought both dignity and elegance to this edition, and given us all a great sense of pride in our work. We are also grateful to John MacCraken for his skillful art direction and mentoring.

To Beth Greenhorn, for photo research and a keen eye, we extend equal admiration and appreciation.

Finally, I wish to offer a very special thanks to Laurel Hyatt for her commitment to excellence, and to Maxine Davidson for her perseverance, humour and grace under pressure. I have been privileged and honoured to work with all these people.

Jonina Wood
Editor-in-Chief, *Canada: A Portrait*

TABLE OF CONTENTS

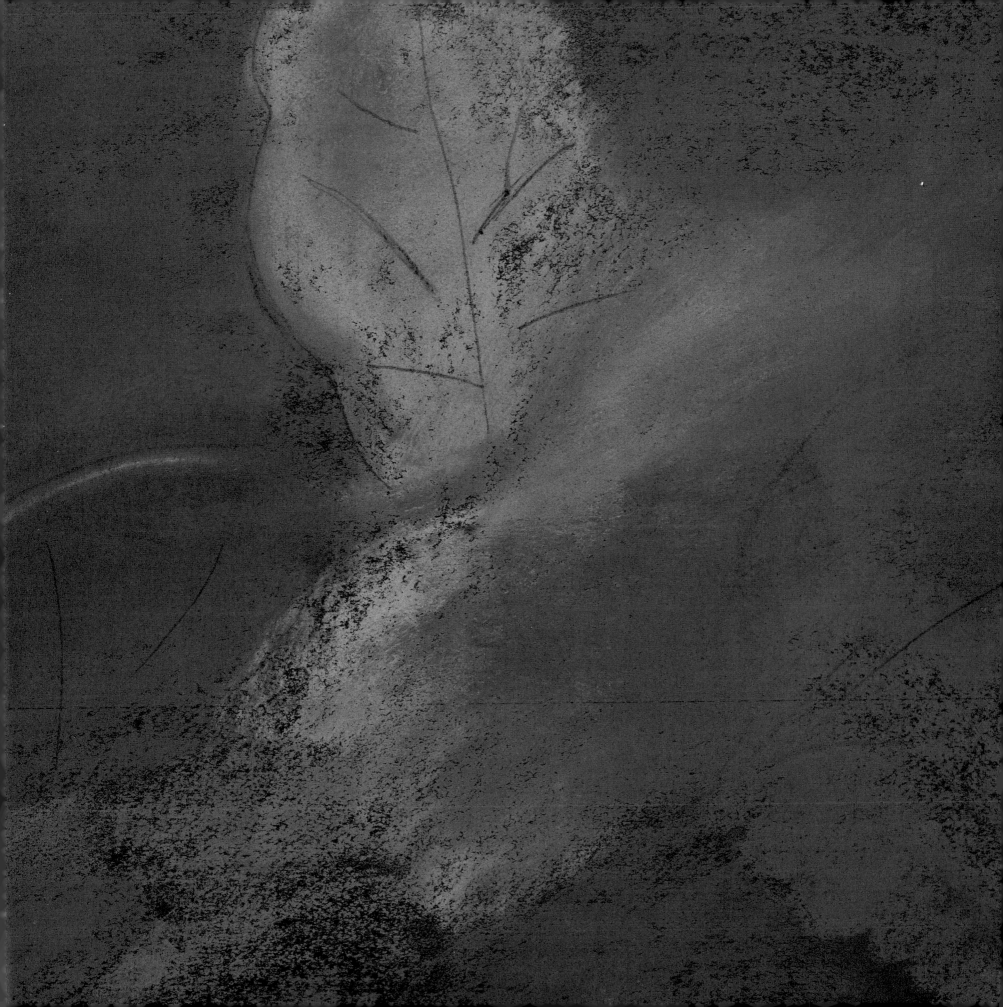

ᓄᓇᕗᑦ ᑐᖅᖢᖕᖎᖃᑕᐅᔨᒪᖑᕐᑦᑐᖅᖡ

VERY FEW OF US HAVE EVER BEEN TO THE ARCTIC AND VERY FEW OF US ACTUALLY

LIVE THERE, BUT IT REMAINS OUR REFUGE, OUR PLACE OF PEACE. OUR LAND OF FEW

FOOTPRINTS.

NOW THAT I LIVE IN TORONTO, IN THE MIDST OF THE CRAZINESS AND PACE OF CITY

LIFE, I FIND MYSELF GOING BACK OFTEN, IN MY MIND, TO THE ARCTIC. TO ITS QUIET.

TO ITS SPACES. TO ITS TRANQUILLITY.

I BELIEVE INNOCENCE ALWAYS SURVIVES. DESPITE THE TROUBLES OF THIS WORLD,

WE CAN ALWAYS SEEK A KIND OF MENTAL REFUGE IN PLACES WE CONNECT WITH

PEACE. CANADA'S ARCTIC IS PART OF OUR COLLECTIVE CONSCIOUSNESS, OUR PLACE

OF INNOCENCE. IT IS A PART OF OUR SPIRITUAL GEOGRAPHY, JUST AS IT IS A PART

OF OUR LAND.

Susan Aglukark, singer

(Opposite page) Inuktitut for "our land of few footprints."

Oxbow, Saskatchewan,

c. 1975.

Photo by Kate Williams.

THE LAND

Of Canada, the legendary Grey Owl once wrote: "I would like to show you this country with its big waters and black forests and little lonely lakes with a wall of trees all around them, that lie so quiet and never move but just look on and on. You know as you go by them that those trees were there ahead of you and will be there after you are dead."

The task of describing the majesty of Canada has been willingly assumed by generations of writers and poets. Its sheer size has posed another challenge. Flying across this country is a "continent's leap," the poet Earle Birney once wrote—we hold "in our morning's hand/the welling and wildness of Canada, the fling of a nation."

For all the imagery of such literary brushstrokes, it is still the clarity of the numbers that completes a portrait of Canada.

This country is vast, wider than the Atlantic Ocean: 5,514 km from west to east, and 4,634 km from south to north. St. John's, Newfoundland is closer to Casablanca in Morocco than it is to Victoria, British Columbia. Vancouver is closer to Mexico City than to Halifax, Nova Scotia. Our coastline is the longest in the world and borders three oceans. Straightened out, it would reach two-thirds of the way to the moon.

Canada's landforms influence our local climates, and often our moods. Our literature is a mirror of the land's mystery and loneliness—scarcely 10% of the country has ever been permanently settled. While our country is the second largest geographical area in the world, only 30 million of us live in a land that covers nearly 10 million km².

Canada's overall population density is barely three people per km², but more than 85% of Canadians live within a 300-km strip along the Canada–United States border. This populated strip thus has a density of 25 people per km²—about the same as that of the United States.

According to some theories, what we now call Canada had its origins some 18,000 years ago. For at least 400,000 years before that, most of it was covered by vast glaciers, some up to four kilometres thick. The few areas that escaped these icefields, in the extreme northwest and in small patches of the southern central plains, became home to Canada's Aboriginal settlers, the first humans to inhabit the northern third of the North American continent.

With the melting of the ice, what would become Canada was gradually revealed. Over time, her spaces became populated by waves of immigrants: Indians, Inuit, Europeans, then peoples from almost every nation on earth. The retreating glaciers left the parent materials for fertile soil. The land was a sea of trees, fish flourished in two million lakes, and the rock itself contained minerals in the five great geological regions of the country.

Canada's five geological regions are the North (the Innuitian Region, the Arctic and the Hudson Bay Lowlands of Nunavut and the Northwest Territories); British Columbia and the Yukon (the Cordillera); the Prairies (the Interior Plains of Alberta, Saskatchewan and Manitoba); the Central region (the Canadian Shield and Great Lakes–St. Lawrence Lowlands of Ontario and Quebec); and the four provinces of the Atlantic (Appalachian) region: New Brunswick, Prince Edward Island, Nova Scotia and Newfoundland and Labrador.

The "passive corporal bulk" of the Shield, as the poet E.J. Pratt called it, makes up almost half of Canada's total area, while the sedimentary arctic regions, plains and lowlands account for a quarter of the country, and the Appalachians and steep ranges of the Cordillera cover the remaining quarter. The immense interaction between Canada's people and these spaces is Canada's continuing story.

The North

For generations, our minds have been seized by the idea of Canada's North—the lodestone to which the world's compasses point. Our national anthem calls on us to defend "the True North strong and free" and we've even devised an index of nordicity which measures our northness in terms of latitude, climate and human activity.

The country's newest territory, Nunavut (which means "our land" in Inuktitut), now recognizes a new form of political self-government for the Inuit of the Eastern Arctic. It has resulted from the largest Aboriginal land claim settlement in Canadian history, one that assigned the administration of nearly 2 million km[2] to the 26,500 people who live there. Created on April 1, 1999 from the former Northwest Territories, Nunavut is larger than the United Kingdom, France, Germany and Spain combined.

In the past, segments of seven Canadian provinces and territories were included in the Northwest Territories. First ceded to Canada in 1870 (the mainland North) and 1880 (the Arctic islands), these territories were the birthplace of most of Manitoba, and all of Saskatchewan, Alberta and the Yukon. Parts were later added to Manitoba, Ontario and Quebec. After the creation of Nunavut, the land area of the remaining Northwest Territories is still enormous—nearly 1.4 million km[2].

The great archipelago of Arctic islands is the area of Canada least known by southerners, largely because it is so difficult to get to. Although Baffin Island is twice the size of Great Britain, it has only 28 settlements, including Iqaluit, the capital of Nunavut. Most islands of the High Arctic are surrounded by frozen sea year-round; ice permanently covers large areas of both land and sea and the winters are fierce. The largest ice caps are found on Ellesmere Island, where they can be more than a kilometre thick and may cover more than 20,000 km[2].

But the North is not all snow and ice, nor is the North one place. The southeast part of the Arctic archipelago is moderated by the North Atlantic ocean and gets more snow than elsewhere in the Arctic. With an average July temperature of only 4° C across the North, the midnight sun is barely warm enough to prompt the sudden display of flowers that carpets the tundra. Vegetation grows so slowly that cart tracks left by Sir Edward Parry's expedition in 1820 were still visible as late as 1978. In the highest latitudes in winter, permanent darkness or twilight shrouds the endless reaches of snow and mountain.

The Arctic mainland, mostly Canadian Shield country, is colder than the islands in winter but warmer than they are in summer, with near-shirtsleeve weather that can climb above 11° C in July.

(Top)
Polar bears, Churchill,
Manitoba.
Photo by Daniel J. Cox,
Tony Stone.

(Middle)
Photo by Tom Walker,
Tony Stone.

(Bottom)
Inuit hunter, Labrador.
Photo copyright
Peter Sibbald, 1999.

Although much of the Arctic is exceptionally dry—low precipitation makes some areas semi-desert—in summer the land is often swampy and wet above the layer of permanently frozen ground, called permafrost. Hundreds of rivers and lakes mark the gently rolling rock and gravel landscape, yet only a few stunted bushes can grow north of the tree line. The Mackenzie Valley, however, is an extension of the great plains to the south. Large parts of the valley are outside the permafrost zone, and spruce, larch, white birch, and jack pine grow in the boreal woodlands.

The 67,500 people of Nunavut and the Northwest Territories—over 60% of them Aboriginal—live in 62 communities. The largest settlements began as mining centres; tourism, government administration, and oil and gas exploration have since added to the importance of towns like Iqaluit, Yellowknife, Hay River, Inuvik and Fort Smith.

Yellowknife has the sunniest summers and coldest winters of any Canadian city and is also the coldest year-round, with an average annual high temperature of –0.8° C. The strongest winds in Canada blow in the North: Resolution Island is home to the highest average wind speed in Canada, at 35.5 km/h.

British Columbia and the Yukon

"The first almighty fact about British Columbia," the naturalist Rod Haig-Brown has said, "is [its] mountains." The mountains of the western Cordillera—stretching up through British Columbia and the Yukon nearly to the Arctic Ocean—are a vital part of the region's history. The area used to be called "the West beyond the West" because its towering mountain ranges stopped westward travel cold. Transportation has been a dominant theme in the development of the province and territory, matched in importance only by the quest for resources, and later by the concentration of the region's wealth in the small southwest corner of the province.

The Yukon is essentially a subarctic plateau, broken intermittently by mountains. The Na-Dene-speaking peoples lived well in this chill territory—fish and the abundant Porcupine caribou herd rarely failed them. They were undisturbed by settlers wanting their land, or colonists stealing their resources. Then, on August 17, 1896, Skookum Jim, Tagish Charley and George Carmack discovered gold on Bonanza Creek, a small tributary of the Klondike River. Within two short years, Dawson—the community at the centre of the gold rush—had grown into the largest Canadian city west of Winnipeg.

But most were to leave the Yukon as penniless as they had come, although the gold rush forever changed the Yukon. Though the decline of the gold fields defeated so many, small communities still formed to support other mineral exploration. The territory was policed, mapped and, in 1942, connected by gravel road to the rest of Canada. Today, 86% of its 31,000 residents are non-Aboriginal, and many work directly or indirectly for the gold, zinc, lead and silver mining companies that open and close with each international economic cycle.

"On the prairie

one can see

the colour of the air."

Emily G. Murphy, *Janey Canuck in the West*

British Columbia's mountains were a formidable barrier to east–west travel until they underwent their own gold rush in 1858. The Rockies, the Columbia ranges, and the Coast Mountains were eventually tamed by the Canadian Pacific Railway in 1885, as a condition of the province's joining Confederation. The bleak high plateaus and warmer valleys in the interior of the province were settled slowly as mines were opened and forestry developed. But it was the tiny amount of good land in the Lower Mainland and the eastern edge of Vancouver Island—less than 3% of the province's area—that attracted the largest population.

Fishing and forestry companies were drawn to Vancouver as it grew into the cultural, educational and financial capital of the province—"the pick of Canada," George Bernard Shaw called it. Although Victoria remained the seat of British Columbia's government, Vancouver grew to become the third-largest metropolitan area in Canada, with a population of 1.9 million.

More than 80% of British Columbia's 4 million residents are urban dwellers and fully 80% of them live in the southwestern region. This has reduced the area of land that can be farmed, one of the major problems of the economic geography of the province. It has less cropland than any province or territory outside the North and the Atlantic provinces. On the other hand, it has about a quarter of Canada's saleable wood growing on 20% of the country's productive forested land.

Extensive forestry has altered the landscape, although the area of replanting now exceeds the area of trees cut. A growing movement to aquaculture is not likely to offset the losses incurred by the rapid declines of salmon stocks and the formerly rich fishing industry. Mining and natural gas production represent 20% of the province's economy.

The Prairies

Prime Minister Sir Charles Tupper called the Prairies "the garden of the world." Recruiting for settlers, the federal government advertised them as "the world's bread basket." The great plains of Alberta, Saskatchewan and Manitoba have lived up to both tags, producing staggering amounts of grain and oilseeds. By 1876, Manitoba had shipped its first exports of Red Fife wheat, a rust-free strain developed in Canada, but rapid expansion of wheat production had to await the completion of the Canadian Pacific Railway.

Good moisture-retaining soil was not the only heritage of the ancient ice sheets and glacial seas that once covered much of the provinces. Rich oil, natural gas and potash deposits rival agriculture as sources of wealth. In 1996, western mineral production (including mineral fuels) was worth $32.6 billion, while all Canadian farms brought in $28.6 billion.

Yet the Prairies are not uniformly generous. The large semi-arid belt of the Palliser Triangle in Alberta and Saskatchewan has led many farmers to ruin. This is where the rains have so often failed, perhaps most notably for seven consecutive years in the 1930s.

As Prairie writer Henry Kreisel wrote, "the sheer physical fact of the prairie" has produced two opposite states of mind: "man, the giant–conqueror, and man, the insignificant dwarf always threatened by defeat." The conqueror mentality is reflected

Old barns

in an Alberta field.

Photo by Richard Hartmier,

First Light.

in the West's political history. Manitoba and Saskatchewan were the sites of two unsuccessful rebellions in 1869–70 and 1885 to assert the rights of nomadic Aboriginal inhabitants over encroaching agricultural settlers from the East. It can also be seen in the distribution of population. Each of the three Prairie provinces has only one or two very large cities, whose economic power dominates the hinterland of small towns, farms and ranches.

Central Canada

Ontario and Quebec together—the great central region of Canada—share some of the most varied landscapes in Canada. Yet, they are dominated by two simple geological facts: the Canadian Shield, whose rugged rocks sweep across the bulk of the region, and the slim fertile belt of the Lower Great Lakes and the St. Lawrence River Valley. In the corridor of cities from Windsor to Québec, more than 50% of Canada's population and nearly 66% of national income are concentrated in barely 2% of Canada's land.

Ontario has more than half of the best agricultural land in the country. From fruit and grapes along the Niagara escarpment to dairy farms in the London–Woodstock area and the Bruce Peninsula, from wheat and barley to beef farms, the province has brought in the largest cash receipts for farm products in every year since at least 1981. The province's quarter-million square kilometres of productive forestlands yield more than a billion dollars' worth of lumber and pulp and paper annually. In northern Ontario, the Shield country is rich in nickel, gold, copper

and zinc. In 1995, the province produced minerals worth more than $5.8 billion.

Ontario is home to the greatest proportion of city-dwellers in Canada—about 82% of Ontarians live in urban areas. Nearly half of the province's 11 million people live in or around Toronto, Hamilton, St. Catharines and Oshawa, and indeed, it is the suburbs that are growing at the expense of the larger cities. Because their cores have permanent residential populations, however, the cities retain their vitality and civility.

Quebec is the "original heart" of Canada, novelist Anne Hébert has said—"the hardest and deepest kernel. The core of first time." The largest province in the country, Quebec's 1.5 million km² cover more than 15% of Canada's surface—more than the United Kingdom, Germany and France combined. As early as the end of the 19th century, Quebec's farms were well known for their pork and dairy products and more than a quarter of Canada's dairy manufacturing operations are located here. About 13% of Canada's total agricultural production takes place in the province, whose farm cash receipts came to more than $4.6 billion in 1996.

The enormous forested areas of the Shield are another significant resource—Quebec has the second-largest area of forestland in the country, after the Northwest Territories. Some 540,000 km² of forest are productive, and the province replaces the cut trees with about 32 million seedlings annually. Quebec is responsible for more than 40% of Canada's paper production, and is among the 10 leading producers of pulp and paper in the world. In the Shield, too, rise the great rivers that have made Quebec the largest producer of hydroelectricity in Canada—about 30% of the national total.

The Atlantic Region

The most heavily forested of all Canadian provinces and territories (proportional to its area) is New Brunswick. More than 80% of the province is covered with trees, while only 5% of the land is suitable for farming. Since the 19th century, timber has dominated the economy. Forestry is the largest natural-resource sector of the province, followed by mining, agriculture (principally potatoes and seed potatoes) and fishing. Tourism now generates more revenue than agriculture.

No place in Nova Scotia is further than 65 km from the ocean. The province has more than 3,000 lakes, 3,800 coastal islands, 100 provincial parks, and more historical sites than any province except Quebec. About 10% of the land is suitable for agriculture, and lumbering is still important—70% of the province is forested, the majority of it in private hands. Offshore oil and natural gas deposits are being exploited, and mining (coal, salt and gypsum) contributes nearly $400 million to the economy annually. Nova Scotia is second only to British Columbia in the value of its fishery, especially scallops and lobsters.

In 1534, explorer Jacques Cartier described Prince Edward Island as "the fairest land that may possibly be seen." With its fertile red soil, nearly half the province's land is highly productive and up to 90% is potentially farmland. Agriculture, notably potato farming, accounts for about $300 million annually.

Newfoundland and Labrador is composed of two distinctly different landforms: the ancient Precambrian rock of the Canadian Shield in the mainland territory of Labrador, and the typically Appalachian forms of the island of Newfoundland. The province is highly urbanized: in 1991, some 76% of Newfoundlanders lived in incorporated towns. At one time, the province's economy was virtually dependent on the fishery, but mining (especially iron ore) and offshore oil are now the major resource-based sectors. The extraordinary wealth of the Voisey Bay mineral discovery has yet to be developed. Because of the poor soil and rigorous climate, agriculture is not significant. Forestry provides both fuel and newsprint.

With the exception of the subarctic areas of northern Labrador, the Atlantic region enjoys a moderate climate with long but not excessively cold winters, and cool summers. New Brunswick's more continental climate is colder in winter in the interior than along the coast. Prince Edward Island, unlike its neighbours, is relatively free of fog year-round, although winter ice in the strait and gulf requires icebreakers to keep the shipping lanes open. Nova Scotia's summer is cool and often foggy, while the autumn is usually clear and long. The island of Newfoundland has cool summers and inland winter temperatures are moderate.

Winter sea conditions can be hazardous, particularly off the coast of Newfoundland; countless ships and lives have been lost over the centuries. St. John's has more days with freezing rain than any other Canadian city, and is the foggiest and windiest. Goose Bay, Labrador is the snowiest place in Canada, receiving 409 cm annually, followed by St. John's with 364 cm.

Great Horned Owl.

Peace River, Alberta.

Photo by Brian Wolitski,

Viewpoints West.

IF I WERE A BEAR Winnie-the-Pooh, known worldwide as a "bear of very little brain," earned his sobriquet from a tiny bear cub that was brought to England by a Canadian soldier in 1914.

Harry Colebourn, an army veterinarian, had set out from his home town of Winnipeg with a trainload of soldiers headed to England to join the war effort. On the way, they stopped in White River, Ontario, and there on the train platform was a young bear cub being offered for sale. Colebourn bought the bear and promptly named her Winnie, after his home town—Winnipeg. His intention was to bring her along to England as the group's mascot.

The exigencies of war soon took over, however, and once in England, Colebourn was forced to drop the little bear at the London Zoo for safekeeping. By the time he returned, four years later, Winnie had become a veritable entertainer for the crowds of adults and children that visited the zoo, among them the young son of the English author Alan Alexander Milne.

The boy was so taken with the young bear that Milne wrote the famous children's story Winnie-the-Pooh and many more stories and poetry about the black bear. Although bears generally don't make it much beyond their 10th birthday in the wild, bears in captivity often live three times as long. Winnie died at the London Zoo, in 1934, of simple old age.

Today, it's estimated that there are about 300,000 black bears in Canada. Elusive creatures, they weather winter well, with their great furry coats. Noting this, Milne wrote a poem called Furry Bear. "If I were a bear," runs the poem, "And a big bear too,/ I shouldn't much care if it froze or snew;/ I shouldn't much mind/ if it snowed or friz—/ I'd be all fur-lined,/ with a coat like his!"

(Left)
Winnie the bear, mascot of the Second Canadian Infantry Brigade, 1914. Harry Colebourn is in the middle row, second from the left.
Photo courtesy the Colebourn family.
"Furry Bear" by A.A. Milne, from *Now We Are Six* by A.A. Milne. Copyright 1927 by E.P. Dutton, renewed © 1955 by A.A. Milne. Used by permission of Dutton Children's Books, a division of Penguin Putnam Inc.

Hunter Hauling a Seal, 1966.
Work by Parr,
Courtesy West Baffin Eskimo
Co-operative Ltd.

SVERDRUP'S AUSUITTUQ In 1930, Canada purchased 259,000 km^2 of its High Arctic islands from the Norwegian explorer Otto Sverdrup for $67,000—the exact cost of his northern expedition. It was a purchase that finally ensured Canada's sovereignty in the Arctic. Although Canada had acquired the Arctic islands from Britain in 1880, we had not established a permanent presence there. Whalers from Scotland and the United States still fished off the islands, while British, American and Norwegian explorers named many of the islands after themselves or their fellow countrymen.

The 1931 Census recorded 13,500 people in the Northwest Territories and Yukon—only about 1 in every 1,000 Canadians. In the intervening years, population density has remained very low: in 1999, there were about 99,000 Northerners, which tells us that about 3 out of every 1,000 Canadians live in the territories.

Sverdrup's sale carried another legacy to Canada. In what is now Nunavut, Canada's most northerly community is Grise Fiord, which is Norwegian for pig fiord. This 150-km^2 hamlet of 148 mostly Inuit people (1996 Census) was given this name by Sverdrup who was reminded of pigs by the grunting of the walruses. The Inuktitut name for the settlement, on the other hand, is Ausuittuq, which means "the place that never thaws out."

WOOLLY SECRETS There is a small creature living in Canada's North known as the Arctic Woolly Bear. This bear, which is actually a caterpillar, spends most of its time frozen and thus could unlock the key to the mysteries of cryopreservation. This is the scientific term applied to the storage of living tissue for later use.

Scientists have discovered that just before winter arrives, the Woolly secretes a kind of internal antifreeze called glycerol, as well as other similar compounds that protect its cells and vital organs during the chill seasons of the Arctic. (Woolly is often called upon to survive a drop in body temperature of 50° C.) Not unreasonably, scientists are extremely curious about how Woolly manages to go into a "deep freeze" and remain alive. They think his secret may eventually tell us how to extend the shelf life of living tissues and even body parts for later use in surgery and other medical procedures.

Science aside, there's an old folklore tradition that says if you see a Banded Woolly Bear, which is another type of woolly caterpillar, in the fall, the width of its black bands will tell you what kind of winter to expect. The narrower the band, the harsher the winter. In Canada, the appearance of this Woolly generally means winter isn't very far away, and his disappearance means it's becoming very, very cold.

(Left)

Arctic Woolly Bear.

Illustration by Neville Smith.

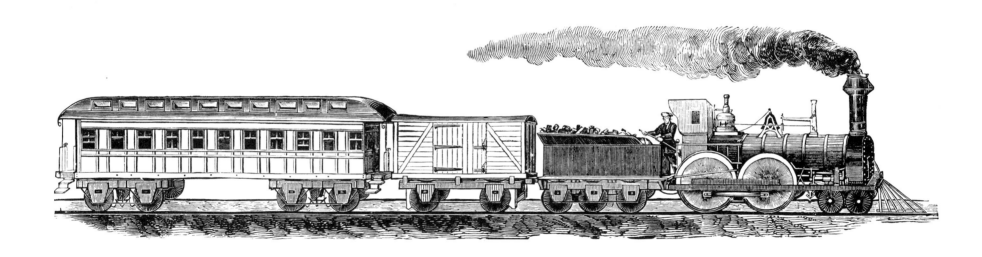

TIME ON HIS HANDS One day in 1876, Sir Sandford Fleming, one of Canada's most respected engineers, waited 12 hours in an Irish railway station because the train schedule failed to indicate the difference between 5:35 p.m. and 5:35 a.m. Frustrated by this experience, Fleming invented Terrestrial Time, a system that divided the day into 24 hours instead of two 12-hour periods, and which would have clocks around the globe set to the same time.

Although his idea was quickly rejected by the "time" authorities of the day, about five years later, Canadian and American railways did adopt universal standard time which divided the globe into 24 equal segments along north–south lines of longitude. In each segment, the time was to be determined by setting clocks to 12 noon as the sun passed directly over a given point. As the sun progressed, therefore, so did the time, depending on where you were on the planet.

Prior to this new time system, there had been no consistency in time standards in Canada. A train traveller going from Halifax to Toronto, for example, could cross five different standards of time so some travellers carried watches with several faces, each set to a local standard.

Today, Canada has six defined time zones: Newfoundland Standard Time (3½ hours behind Greenwich Mean Time); Atlantic Standard Time (4 hours behind); Eastern Standard Time (5 hours behind); Central Standard Time (6 hours behind); Mountain Standard Time (7 hours behind); and Pacific Standard Time (8 hours behind).

Canada's Climate

Canada's is a continental temperate climate, which means that we have warm summers and cold winters. Of course, there are great regional variations—some parts of British Columbia have a mild climate, while the Prairies have created an entire literature based around their extremes of temperature. From summers of brilliant sun and deep blue skies, cooled by westerly winds, to fierce winters, each Prairie season brings its own lyric charms: a sighting of the northern lights can be an awe-inspiring event.

In eastern Canada, the climate is somewhat milder. Ontario has its hot, sometimes humid summers, and its cold, snowy winters, but generally not with the same vigour as is found on the Prairies.

The place with the most extreme climate in Canada is the former weather station at Isachsen, in what is now Nunavut, with a Climate Severity Index of 99 out of 100. Canada must be one of the few places in the world with an official measure of misery— Environment Canada's Climate Severity Index, which rates the climate of various cities in terms of human comfort and well-being.

As it turns out, Canada's toughest climates are not all in the North. St. John's, Newfoundland, has a higher Climate Severity Index than either Yellowknife in the Northwest Territories or Whitehorse, Yukon. For capital cities, going from most severe to least, the index values measured at each airport are: Iqaluit (76), St. John's (59), Yellowknife (57), Québec (52), Winnipeg (51), Regina (49), Charlottetown (48), Halifax (47), Whitehorse (46), Ottawa (44), Edmonton (43), Fredericton (41), Toronto (36) and Victoria (15).

Undeniably, climate has influenced where we live and even how we make our livings. Early First Nations migration and settlement were influenced by the warmth of seacoasts and seas that supported fish and sea mammals, and of forests and grasslands that were home to animals that provided food and hides. The agriculture and pasture that sustained European settlement were largely dependent on good soils and climates with an adequate growing season and necessary moisture.

For farming, climate has a huge impact. The commercial development of early-maturing Marquis wheat by 1911, for example, meant that much larger areas of the prairies could be opened and farmed despite the short growing season. Canola is now a major crop in the

West because the cool nights and hot sunny days produce a seed with high oil content. In 1998, crop receipts of $2.8 billion for canola exceeded those for wheat for the first time. Commercial forestry, too, is influenced by climate—warmth and good soil are needed for growing trees, while wind and thunderstorms can spark forest fires.

Canadians also rely on predictable weather patterns. For example, snow fills reservoirs for hydroelectric power and sets the stage for winter sports. Even small variations can have large economic consequences. About a third of the energy we use—and we are the world's largest consumers of energy, per capita—goes to offset the cold of winter. Each centimetre of snow raises fuel consumption for cars and trucks by 50%. On the other hand, a winter that is two to three degrees warmer than usual can save the equivalent of 45 million barrels of oil.

Extremes Few events colour our memory so much as great natural catastrophes—again, in large part, products of our climate. The drought years of the 1930s, for instance, are a permanent part of the folklore of the western provinces because the rain failed from 1929 to 1937. Nearly a quarter of Canada's arable land was affected—more than 7 million hectares. Wind erosion of the soil compounded the problem. In Saskatchewan, two-thirds of the province's rural population was forced to turn to government relief because of the crop failures and low prices for wheat.

Floods, too, have had a devastating power. Caused by runoff after heavy rains, and compounded by snowmelt in early spring, British Columbia's Fraser River flood in 1948 displaced 16,000 people. The largest floods in recent times have both struck Manitoba: the Red River flood of May 1950, during which 100,000 Winnipeggers were evacuated; and the flood of April and May 1997 that covered 1,950 km² in water—an area one-third the size of Prince Edward Island.

Global Warming Scientists now know that the surface of the earth has been warming gradually since the last century—an average temperature increase of 0.3° to 0.6° C world-wide over the past 90 years, and an increase of 1.1° C in Canada. The concentrations of some trace gases that may influence surface climate (the so-called "greenhouse" gases) are also increasing globally. Measurements suggest that rain and snowfall have increased about 10% in Canada between 1955 and 1980. This global warming—stronger here than in many other countries—may mean a real change in climate, or it may simply be a normal large-scale fluctuation.

(Top)

Mountain view.

Photo by Harry Savage.

(Middle)

Loon,

Lake of the Woods, Ontario.

Photo by Tom Thomson.

(Bottom)

Marram Grass,

Miscou Island,

New Brunswick.

Photo by John Sylvester,

First Light.

According to Environment Canada, global warming could potentially mean that Canada would be 5° to 10° warmer in 100 years—up to three times the increase in the average temperature worldwide. Winters and summers would be warmer, with increased precipitation (especially rain) and heat waves. Farming might benefit from the warming trend, while fishing would likely be better in some areas of the country and harmed in others.

Thus, the Canadian government joined 150 other nations in signing the 1992 United Nations Framework Convention on Climate Change. The Convention aims to have developed countries like Canada reduce their greenhouse gas emissions to 1990 levels as soon as possible. While progress is slow, Canada is committed to reporting publicly on what measures we are taking and how we are doing.

Air Quality Canada has never had the kind of week-long smog that killed 4,000 people in England in 1952, but Toronto's five-day Grey Cup smog in November 1962 did result in increased hospital admissions and postponed the football game. Both smogs were the result of burning carbon-based fuels like coal, oil, natural gas and gasoline, combined with still air. The federal government and most provinces now have clean air laws that establish air-quality and pollution emission standards. Some cities issue smog alerts and pollution warnings. Regulations to limit emissions have had a positive effect on air quality, through better-designed car engines and exhaust systems, filters on industrial smokestacks, and cleaner industrial processes.

Ozone depletion is a particularly hazardous problem. Released chemicals called chloro-fluorocarbons are thinning the protective ozone layer above the earth, letting in more harmful ultraviolet-B radiation from the sun. The radiation can cause reduced crop yields, slow down the growth of forests, and will likely result in increased skin cancer rates. At a United Nations conference in 1987, Canada joined many other nations in agreeing to reduce the release of such chemicals by 50% by 2000.

Not all air pollution is the fault of industry, vehicles and household heating. When Mount Pinatubo erupted in 1991—the largest volcanic eruption in the 20th century—it spewed so much dust and gas that global temperatures fell slightly during the next two years as these airborne substances blocked solar radiation. Dust storms such as those on the Prairies in the 1930s are a source of airborne substances, as are forest fires and the swamps and wetlands that emit methane and volatile organic compounds.

Water Canada has 9% of the world's renewable supply of fresh water and most of us take safe water for granted. But growing cities and their sewage treatment plants are putting pressure on our supplies of clean water. Two major Canadian cities—Victoria and Halifax—still discharge raw sewage into the sea.

Chemicals that pollute the water include mercury, DDT and dioxins. In 1970, members of two Ojibwa bands in Ontario—the Grassy Narrows band and the Islington band on the Whitedog Reserve—were poisoned when they ate fish contaminated by mercury from a local

Hutterite woman throws building scraps out during the expansion of the Wolf Creek Colony, near Stirling, Alberta. Photo by William DeKay.

pulp and paper mill. Water itself is a powerful natural force, capable of decomposing rocks and soil, and eroding shorelines, and violent events such as storms and flooding can also affect water quality.

Recycling helps reduce the amount of garbage going into Canadian dumps, from which chemicals can leach into the groundwater. In 1994, more than two-thirds of Canadian households had access to paper, glass, plastic and tin-can recycling programs, and more than 80% took part in the programs.

Plants and Animals "Save Furbish's lousewort" may never become a popular cry, but this rare Atlantic plant may well deserve as much attention as some of nature's more cuddly specimens. Along with 213 other plants, the lowly lousewort is imperilled, and another 800 species are listed as rare—nearly a third of Canada's 3,300 native plants. Most provinces have laws protecting endangered species, but it requires the concerted attention of the public as well as botanists to save these threatened plants.

More familiar are the birds, animals and reptiles that are threatened or endangered, such as the whooping crane, the sea otter and the peregrine falcon. We know that several species are officially extinct, including the sea mink, the Labrador duck (last seen in 1878), the passenger pigeon (1914), and the blue walleye (1965). Most disappeared forever because of hunting, overfishing and egg-gathering. Several others are on the edge of extinction. Some species have been extirpated—that is, they are no longer found in Canada, but may possibly survive elsewhere—such as the black-footed ferret, the swift fox and the timber rattlesnake.

Habitat protection and public attention are the most useful ways of preventing further losses. The habitat of the rare Acadian whitefish (discovered in 1967) must be protected because the fish only lives in one small stream. Spawning grounds must be kept clear of sediment and chemicals. Parks such as Saskatchewan's Grasslands National Park protect nesting areas, and the extirpated greater prairie-chicken has been sighted again. Falcons, whose eggs were damaged by DDT, are slowly gaining in number now that use of the pesticide has been banned.

Parks and protected areas are conservation sites for endangered plants and animals. Canada's national and provincial park systems both began in 1885, in Banff and Niagara Falls. National parks make up nearly 2% of the country's land mass. Fifteen Canadian parks and park reserves have now been designated World Heritage sites by the United Nations Educational, Scientific and Cultural Organization.

WHEN I'M ASKED, AS I SOMETIMES AM, TO DEFINE A CANADIAN, I REPLY THAT

CANADIANS ARE GRADUALISTS. BY THAT I MEAN THAT THEY DON'T JUMP TO SUDDEN

CONCLUSIONS, THAT THEY'VE LEARNED THE ART OF COMPROMISE, AND, UNLIKE THEIR

NEIGHBOURS, THEY DON'T LIVE BY THE GUN.

CANADIANS DEVELOPED GRADUALLY, NOT BY REVOLUTION, AND HAVE BEEN SUSTAINED

BY A REVERENCE FOR ORDER, NOT BY CIVIL WAR. THAT'S WHY WE'VE BECOME

PEACEMAKERS TO THE WORLD.

THIS HAS ALWAYS BEEN A LAND OF IMMIGRANTS — A POLYGLOT COUNTRY IN WHICH WE

HAVE HAD TO LEARN TO GET ALONG WITH THE STRANGERS WHO ARRIVE ON OUR SHORES.

WE'VE BEEN CALLED THE PEACEABLE KINGDOM — A GOOD TITLE IN MY VIEW.

Pierre Berton, author

Place Jacques Cartier,
Montréal, Quebec.
Photo by Pierre St-Jacques,
Imagination.

THE PEOPLE

1900 It was the year the Montreal Shamrocks won the Stanley Cup. Men wore high-collared shirts, collared vests and homburgs. Many sported waxed moustaches and carried walking sticks. Women's fashions leaned to long skirts, often with accentuated waists. Blouses had full sleeves, and hats and bonnets were trimmed with ribbons and feathers. It was 1900 and Canada was 33 years old.

Now a dominion from sea to sea, Canada had just built a national railway, sent troops to a foreign war in Africa and even discovered gold in the Yukon.

Truly, these were heady days. Canada was a young nation of just 5.4 million people, and with a young population, one-third of which were under the age of 15. Most people still lived in the country, less than two out of five in cities. Families tended to be large, and large also on family values. The average household held about five people.

Outside the home, Canadian pastimes included cycling, riding, boating and skating. Indoors, the piano in the parlour provided a certain merriment, at least for those families who could afford it. Interior décor featured heavy laces and brocades, supported by the use of marble and dark woods. Fashionable homes boasted verandas and Victorian, romantic or gothic façades.

Ethnically, a little under one in three people was French and just under three in five were British, but a new development was about to dramatically shift this landscape. Prime Minister Wilfrid Laurier and his Minister of the Interior, Clifford Sifton, were keen to bring in immigrants—"a lot of immigrants." People who would settle the West and help put to rest the fear of American annexation. Settlers who would buy the products of new factories in Quebec and Ontario and provide the country's new railway with much needed passengers.

Mid-century

Although the Detroit Red Wings won the Stanley Cup in 1950, hockey was still Canada's game. Even Barbara Ann Scott supported our hegemony on ice, winning world and Olympic figure skating championships in 1947 and 1948. In terms of the fashion of the day, men wore more subdued suits with simpler lines; long but slim skirts were the fashion for women. Teenage girls sported saddle shoes and boys were beginning to make fashion statements with "drape-shape" slacks. The zoot suit was in.

In Canada, as throughout the Western world, the 1950s followed a decade of depression and six years of world war. With this now behind them, Canadians were generally imbued with a sense of optimism about life and the future. Newfoundland had just joined the country, prospectors had struck oil in Alberta and the Royal Canadian Air Force had just flown the first non-stop flight across the country.

Returning veterans and new immigrants were being housed and integrated into the labour force. Wartime rationing had ended and consumer goods such as automobiles and radios were now readily available. Electricity was being extended to rural and farm areas. Streetcars were beginning to disappear, giving way to the buses that would replace them in many cities.

By 1950, Canada's population was close to 14 million, more than two-and-a-half times its level in 1900. The proportion of children in the population had fallen to less than 30% while the percentage of elderly had risen to about 8%.

Canada was increasingly urban. Three out of five people now lived in cities and towns. Although fertility had fallen during the Depression, it was now on the rise and would eventually constitute a full-scale baby boom. The advent of veterans' housing projects marked the beginning of tract housing, sub-divisions and suburbia. Homes were compact and utilitarian and average household size had dropped from five to four people.

In spite of all this energy and change, there was a darker side. In 1950, a national rail strike silenced industry, and in the summer of the same year, there had been a major flood in Manitoba's Red River Valley. A polio epidemic was running riot through much of Canada. The Korean War had just broken out, bringing fear of another world conflict and, even more menacing, the possible use of nuclear weapons. The "Cold War," as it was called in reference to the chill between the Soviet bloc and the Western world, was in full, chilling swing.

In the midst of all this, a new wave of immigrants arrived in Canada, the result of persons displaced by the Second World War. The statisticians of the day viewed this happily, projecting that Canada's population at the end of the 20th century would be something like 15 million people. They were wrong by a factor of two.

Canada Today

Canada, at the end of the 20th century, is a nation of some 30 million people. Although

the early predictions did not refer to our aging, we are nonetheless a much older population: only 20% of us are now 15 and under.

We are highly citified. About one in three Canadians now lives in the country's four largest metropolitan areas. Body art—tattooing and piercing—seems to have moved from the social fringes to the mainstream. Go to any concert in the late 1990s and the range of sartorial splendour runs the gamut from tuxedos to jeans. Hemlines are absolutely unpredictable: some have joked that they rise and fall with the same cadence as the stock market.

Our perception of time has changed as well. In 1867, the intrepid traveller undertaking a sojourn from Ottawa to the West Coast would have needed from 32 to 64 days. In 1900, a traveller might have managed the same distance in four to eight days on the country's new rail system. Today, anyone can hop a plane in Ottawa and be in Vancouver five hours later. Yet, ironically, for all this saving of time, most Canadians report they have "no time."

Urban Tiara Most of us live within 200 km of our southern border. In fact, the lights of our major cities form a kind of urban tiara, with Montréal and Toronto at the centre and St. John's and Victoria on either end. Quebec and Ontario are the central and also the most populous provinces, but the West Coast has a larger population than that of the eastern seaboard. Growth in the East is slow and hampered by a westward migration, a trend captured well in Donald Shebib's classic film, *Goin' Down the Road*. Ontario, and in particular the metropolis of Toronto, is a magnet for Easterners in search of better job prospects,

(Far left)
Wedding in Joly, Quebec.
Photo by Serge Laurin,
courtesy Canadian Museum
of Contemporary
Photography.

(Left)
Nawoki and Miyoko
Takeuchi, Vancouver,
British Columbia,
September 5, 1936.

(Bottom left)
Toronto, Ontario,
April, 1963.
Photo by Michael Semak,
NFB Collection, courtesy
Canadian Museum of
Contemporary Photography.

(Right)
Mrs. Carling, Ottawa,
Ontario, c. 1930.
Photo by Jules Alexandre
Castonguay, courtesy
National Archives of
Canada, PA-133239.

Bert and George in the
living room, 1973.
Photo by Barbara Astman,
Jane Corkin Gallery, in the
collection of the Canadian
Museum of Contemporary
Photography.

but Ontario, and indeed Quebec, lose some migrants to British Columbia.

On the other hand, there has been little new migration to the Atlantic provinces throughout much of this century. This has had the cultural effect of tying these areas to their collective past. Acadian, Gaelic and Loyalist roots go deep in the region and continue to be reflected in the music, architecture and even demeanour of the people. For example, the architecture of the Acadian ancestral homes that line Nova Scotia's Fundy Shore seems to be a reflection of a hardworking, pragmatic people.

Migration aside, both language and architecture have a say in the landscape of Canada. Montréal is known for its outdoor wrought-iron staircases and Québec for its ancient fortifications and city walls, which speak visually to a different cultural heritage. Quebec, with about one-quarter of the nation's population, is the linguistic centre of French Canada but there are people whose mother tongue is French who live in other regions, particularly in Ontario and New Brunswick.

Nowhere in Canada has the change in family values been more pronounced than in Quebec, where birth rates fell from the highest in the country to the lowest between the 1950s and the 1980s. Today, they are close to the national level, but Quebeckers have also led nationally in the switch from church or civil marriage to common-law marriage. In 1996, some 43% of all common-law couples in Canada lived in Quebec.

A full 40% of all Canadians live in Ontario, a province so vast that it can take three days to drive from Ottawa in the east to its western border between Kenora and Winnipeg. The huge metropolis that sprawls around Toronto is a constant centre of change as it absorbs migrants from other parts of Canada and from around the world. In so doing, it has become one of the most eclectic areas in the country, if not the world, in terms of its ethnic, linguistic and cultural life.

Certainly, Toronto's growth now rivals that of the Prairies, where in the early 1900s, immigration led to such an enormous ethnic diversity. In Winnipeg's Elmdale Cemetery, for instance, the names on the headstones of early pioneers are French, English, Polish, Ukrainian, Russian, German, and Lithuanian. In the city beyond the cemetery gates, their descendants go about their daily routines, gathering in cafés and donut shops, reading the same papers, watching the same television programs and sometimes draping themselves in Canadian flags at the same critical hockey games.

Yet, in the wake of one of the largest population influxes in Canada's history (that of the early 1900s), today, fewer than 17% of all Canadians can call Manitoba, Saskatchewan or Alberta home.

In British Columbia, places such as California, Hawaii, China, Japan, India and Australia seem closer in spirit, if not in fact, than does eastern Canada. People of Asian ancestry now dominate in neighbourhoods where, until the 1930s, restrictive covenants prevented them from so much as owning land. (Legislation and social pressures in the province also prevented Asians from voting, serving in elected office or in the public service or practising professions such as law and pharmacy.) Similarly, other provinces, such as Quebec, Nova Scotia and Saskatchewan, formerly prohibited white women from

working in firms owned by Asians. Today, in British Columbia, with some 13% of the total Canadian population, less than one in five is a member of a visible minority.

In the Territories, our history has been dramatically different. Perhaps the sheer size of its land mass has caused a different culture to prevail. With a population of less than 100,000 people, if this area was divided equally, each resident would have over 37 km^2 to him or herself. Just this remoteness has enabled Aboriginal residents to maintain more of their traditions and their languages than Aboriginal peoples living elsewhere. Now, with the new territory known as Nunavut, the Inuit have fulfilled a long-held dream to control their own political and economic life.

Immigration

Undeniably, Canada is an immigrant nation. Search any family tree and our immigrant roots quickly reveal themselves. Even our first peoples, the Aboriginals, tell stories of their ancestors arriving on the back of a turtle or by the trickery of Raven. The French came just after 1600. Yankee and British traders arrived around 1760. The United Empire Loyalists took up residence after the American Revolution and more Scots came along in the early 1800s, driven off their land at home. The Irish came to escape the potato famines of the 1840s.

In the 1960s, the daughter of an immigration officer, Gabrielle Roy, wrote that Canadians "have accepted suffering that [has come] from elsewhere and [let it become] a source of enrichment for us. Out of this human diversity, out of the melancholy of the exile, as well as his happier side as exemplified in his songs and dances, our country [has] slowly [taken] shape."

Today, onion domes and minarets shape part of the outline of our cityscapes and the perogies, cabbage rolls, cannelloni, bok choy and chow mein of later immigrants have joined the wild rice, maize, tourtière and Yorkshire pudding of earlier settlers on the menus of the land. Somewhere between the earlier legislation that discriminated against Chinese and Japanese people and the writing of Gabrielle Roy, Canada has matured and grown up.

Today, most of us are born Canadian, but are the children of immigrant parents or ancestors. About 17% of Canadians today have emigrated from another country. Those born in Europe were most likely to have come before 1971. In the 1960s, changes in immigration policy removed many of the barriers to non-European immigrants. Since 1991, Asia has been the major source of newcomers. Approximately three-fifths of all those who came to Canada from 1991 through the first five months of 1996 were born in some part of Asia.

Visible minorities represent a little more than 11% of the population. Most live in the largest urban centres, forming 32% of the population in the census metropolitan area of Toronto, 31% in that of Vancouver and 16% in that of Calgary. In Edmonton, Montréal, Ottawa–Hull and Winnipeg, visible minorities make up anywhere from 11% to 14% of the population.

"Canada has never been a melting pot; it is more like a tossed salad."

Arnold Edinborough

(Top)
Maurice, 1939.
Work by Lilias Torrence
Newton, courtesy Hart House
Permanent Collection,
University of Toronto.

(Right)
Girl in Black Jacket,
c. 1950.
Work by Jack Humphrey,
courtesy National Gallery
of Canada.

Our Languages

English or French is the mother tongue of most Canadians—that is, the language they first learned in childhood and still understand. Only about 16% of our population speak a non-official language as their mother tongue. Of these, Chinese, Italian and German are the most prevalent.

More than 2.5 million Canadians may be found speaking a language at home other than English or French. This includes 500,000 people who speak Chinese at home and somewhere under 250,000 who speak Italian. Punjabi, Spanish, Portuguese, Polish, German and Vietnamese are other languages that are commonly heard in Canadian homes, while about 50,000 persons routinely speak Cree.

Immigrants have also brought new religions to Canada. Temples and mosques have joined churches and synagogues on the urban street scene. The number of people who are either Roman Catholic or Protestant continues to decline as a proportion of the total population. On the other hand, the proportion of people who report an affiliation with Islam, Buddhism, Hinduism and Sikhism is increasing.

In a single decade, the number of all Canadians who say they have no connections to a religious organization has almost doubled, from 7% in 1981 to just under 13% in 1991.

Despite the move away from organized religion, Canadians who do attend religious services every week report living happier, less stressful lives. Surveys have shown they also attach a greater importance to marriage and family life than those who do not attend.

Those who attend services are less likely to suffer the dissolution of their marriages and more likely to express the view that women prefer home and children to paid work.

Family Life

Open any page of the "Canadian family album" and you will surely find mother, father, children, Buddy the dog and Minou the cat. But this halcyon image, rooted in our collective past, has become somewhat blurred by the realities of today. Canadian households are now about half the size they were 100 years ago. The size of families has also been falling since 1966 when it was just under four persons. In 1997, the average family size was three.

Even within the families that we might think of as "traditional" with a mother, father and children, we now find an increasing number of blended families, with children from previous marriages or unions. A couple may have "her" children, "his" children and then "their" children.

At the turn of the century, the 1901 Census recorded fewer than 700 divorced people in the entire country. In 1951, the Census reported nearly 32,000 divorced people, which was less than 1% of the adult population. In 1996, the Census found that over 7% of the adult population was divorced: that same year, nearly 72,000 divorces were issued.

Still, most Canadians live in families. In fact, in 1996, over one-half of all Canadians were spouses or lone parents in families. One-third were children in families. Only about 13% of Canadians were not living as part of a family

"I didn't know at first that there were two languages in Canada. I just thought there was one way to speak to my father and another way to speak to my mother."

Louis St. Laurent

"I am French

I am English

And I am Métis

But more than this

Above all this

I am a Canadian

and proud to be free."

Duke Redbird, poet

and a large proportion of them (7 in 10) were living alone.

Most of Canada's children live in a family with both their biological parents, while about one in five live in a family with only one parent and about 1 in 10 under the age of 12 live in a blended family. More than 55% of young children—those under six years old—live in families with both parents working, while for just under 60% of children living in a lone-parent family, that parent works.

Talk about a time crunch. In the course of a week, the average Canadian adult spends about 10.5 hours a day sleeping, eating and on other personal care. Those with paying jobs spend about 50 hours a week on the job and just getting to and from work.

About 90% of Canadians spend a good 30 hours a week on housework, home maintenance and repair, primary childcare and volunteer work. Canadian women still do most of the work in the home, but men are doing more. Surveys now show that more than 50% of married men who work outside the home also provide care for their children or perform household chores such as cleaning and cooking.

There is some argument about whether modern labour-saving devices in the home have really made household work easier. For example, yes, we may now have automatic washers and dryers but we now launder many garments that were once picked up by the local dry-cleaning service.

At Home In 1900, we might have had a piano in the parlour and that was the focus of our entertainment and fun. In 1950, we might have had a console radio in the living room

(a few years later a TV). Today, (1997) more than half of Canadian homes have three or more radios or two or more colour televisions. One in five homes has two or more VCRs and well over one in three a personal computer. Close to two-fifths of all homes have three or more telephones and almost one in five a cellular phone.

Nevertheless, such distractions and innovative household equipment take a relatively small part out of our income. Personal taxes are our largest expenditure, over one-fifth of the total annual average household expenditure of almost $50,000. Shelter takes an average of just over 17%, followed by transportation and food at about 12% each.

Approximately 6 out of 10 Canadian households own their homes. Among young homeowners (under the age of 30), about 9 out of 10 have a mortgage. On the other hand, about 9 out of 10 homeowners 65 years and older are mortgage-free.

In 1900, there were about a million homes in Canada; in the 1950s, almost 3.5 million. Today, there are nearly 11 million.

Most of us have a strong attachment to home and place, but a fairly large proportion of us do pack up and move. Between 1991 and 1996, about 43% of us moved from one home to another. Of those who moved, most didn't move far. Just over one-half stayed within the same municipality and just less than one-third changed municipalities but stayed within the same province. Approximately 8% of all movers went to another province and another 8% came from another country.

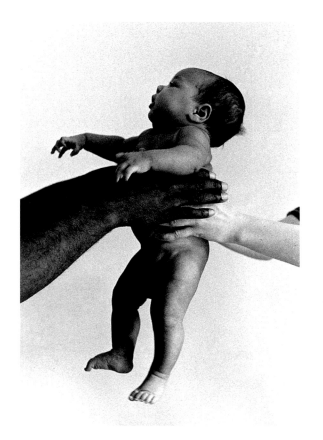

(Far left)
Montréal, Quebec, 1969.
Photo by Gabor Szilasi,
courtesy Canadian Museum
of Contemporary
Photography.

(Middle)
Hallowe'en mouse, Willard
Avenue, Toronto, Ontario,
1991.
Photo by Rob Allen
Photography.

(Left)
Photo by Walter Curtin,
courtesy Canadian Museum
of Contemporary
Photography.

(Top right)
Dresden, Ontario.
Photo by Larry Towell,
Magnum Photos.

(Bottom right)
Banjo faces off with
Copernicus, Lambton
County, Ontario.
Photo by Larry Towell,
Magnum Photos.

Near Verwood,
Saskatchewan, 1994.
Photo by George Webber.

SUBURBAN TALES

"The name of the subdivision was Garden Place, and its streets were named for flowers. On either side of the road the earth was raw; the ditches were running full. Planks were laid across the open ditches, planks approached the doors of the newest houses. The new, white and shining houses, set side by side in long rows in the wound of the earth . . . Last year, just at this time, in March, the bulldozers had come in to clear away the brush and the second-growth and great trees of the mountain forest; in a little while the houses were going up among the boulders, the huge torn stumps, the unimaginable upheavals of that earth. The houses were frail at first, skeletons of new wood standing up in the dusk of the cold spring days. But the roofs went on, black and green, blue and red, and the stucco, the siding; the windows were put in, and plastered with signs that said, Murry's Glass, French's Hardwood Floors; it could be seen that the houses were real. People who would live in them came out and tramped around in the mud on Sundays."

In this excerpt from "The Shining Houses," Canadian author Alice Munro writes about a familiar Canadian phenomenon, the rapid development of suburbia. She contrasts the clean lines of a new housing development as it encroaches on the "disorder and the steep, unmatched angles of roofs and lean-tos" of the "surviving houses" at the edge of town.

"The Shining Houses" was included in Alice Munro's first collection of short stories, entitled *The Dance of the Happy Shades*. Munro has won three Governor General's Awards for her writing. Her 1998 collection of stories, *The Love of a Good Woman*, earned her the Giller Prize.

"MUKLUK" IS INUKTITUT

Most speakers of Canadian English may not realize it, but *hurricane*, *tomato*, *potato* and *mukluk* are all words from indigenous North American languages. In fact, English is rich with words borrowed from the languages of Aboriginal people. *Skunk* and *raccoon*, for example, are Algonquian.

Canada has about 50 Aboriginal languages. At least half of these are either close to extinction (that is, beyond hope of revival) or are endangered. For endangered languages, survival depends on community interest and concerted educational programs. Notably, the Tlingit, Kutenai and Haida families of language are classified as endangered. (In 1996, these languages were the mother tongue of only 500 people.) On the other hand, Cree, Inuktitut, and Ojibway, the strongest of Canada's Aboriginal languages, still thrive—each of these languages is the mother tongue of more than 20,000 people.

Cree is by far the most widely spoken Aboriginal language in Canada; close to 88,000 persons spoke it as their mother tongue in 1996. There are also less widely spoken Aboriginal languages that remain viable, such as Montagnais–Naskapi, which is the mother tongue of 9,000 people in Labrador and Northern Quebec.

(Far left)
Stoney Indian mother with child, Kootenay Plains, 1907.
Photo by Elliot Barnes, courtesy Whyte Museum of the Canadian Rockies, V48/NA66-1582.

(Left)
Photo copyright Peter Sibbald, 1999.

CANADA'S TITANIC Eighty-five years after the largest, "most luxurious

ocean liner" hit an iceberg off Newfoundland and sank to the bottom of the

ocean, the film *Titanic* (by Canadian moviemaker James Cameron) grossed

$2.8 billion at the box office—more than any other movie in history.

But just two years after the Titanic sank, a similar marine disaster attracted far

less attention. In the early hours of May 29, 1914, the *Empress of Ireland*,

a 14,000-ton ocean liner of the same era as the *Titanic*, sank in the Gulf of

St. Lawrence. It was Canada's most devastating marine disaster.

The *Empress* was bound for Liverpool on her 96th voyage with nearly 1,500

people on board. During the *Empress'* first night out from Québec's harbour, in

heavy fog, the Norwegian collier *Storstad*, bearing a load of Cape Breton coal

bound for Montréal, struck her on her starboard side.

In a remarkable twist of fate, a Liverpool man who had served as a fireman aboard

the *Titanic* and now on the *Empress*, survived both shipwrecks to say: "The *Titanic*

went down straight like a baby goes to sleep. The *Empress* rolled over like a hog in

a ditch."

Compared with the nearly two-and-a-half hours it took for the *Titanic* to plunge to

the depths of the ocean, the ill-fated *Empress* went down in just 14 minutes. Only

463 people survived.

The remains of this once elegant and ornate ship lay in less than 50 metres of

water in the Gulf of St. Lawrence near Rimouski until discovered by divers in 1964.

Threatened by plunderers, the *Empress of Ireland* was declared a protected cultural

site in April 1998 by the Quebec government.

TOLSTOY IN WINNIPEG

"Winnipeg is sometimes reminiscent of a Russian city—sleigh traffic, wooden houses, wide streets. Only they have electric trams and electric lighting, and a maze of telephone wires . . . In Halifax the temperature went down to -54° C—even vodka would freeze. They say, though, that this winter is exceptional. Granted, the cold is easier to take here—the air is very dry. Still, I feel very sad that the Doukhobors have moved to such a cold climate.

The whole time [I was in Winnipeg] it was frosty, but calm and sunny. In March during the day puddles form on the streets and give off steam, since the air is quite dry. Transportation along the streets is almost exclusively by tram, if not on foot. Only once in a while does one see tall two-horse sleighs. There are few coachmen, and they can be hired only on special order and for a substantial fare. The sleighs and people in sheepskin coats—a common sight on the streets: Galicians, Doukhobors and others—all this is somewhat reminiscent of Russian cities. But one feels the pulse of life beating more strongly here: more energy, more wealth."

Excerpted from accounts by the eldest son of Leo Tolstoy, this passage describes Sergej Tolstoy's sojourn to Winnipeg in 1899. Sergej accompanied a group of more than 7,000 Doukhobors emigrating from Russia to help them settle in the new "promised land" of Canada. The settlers, who had been persecuted in their homeland for their religion and their pacifist principles, helped open up the Canadian Prairies and half the world's Doukhobors now live in Western Canada. "Doukhobor" is Russian for "spirit wrestler."

STRANGERS WITHIN OUR GATES

"Let me tell you of one little foreign girl. She lives in a room in a disreputable old tenement—one of those human warrens which are multiplying with great rapidity in our city. Her father has no work. The men boarders have no work. The place is incredibly filthy. The little girl has been ill for months—all that time living on the bed in which three or four persons must sleep and which also serves the purpose of tables and chairs . . . Is there not some man or some woman who has a heart and a head who will help that child?"

This passage comes from a letter written to a newspaper by J. S. Woodsworth in the early 1900s. Woodsworth, a Methodist minister who eventually became a Member of Parliament and the first leader of the CCF Party (the forerunner of the NDP), was concerned about the plight of newcomers to Canada and their impact here. In *Strangers Within Our Gates*, a book he wrote on this issue, Woodsworth articulated these public sentiments of the time.

Since the beginning of this century, large numbers of new Canadians have made this country their home. In 1911, for the first time in its history, Canada opened its gates to more than 330,000 immigrants in a single year. Our total population at the time was 7.2 million. Two years later, immigration peaked at 400,000.

In 1951, Canada welcomed 194,000 immigrants, against a total population of 14 million. In 1999, with our population topping 30 million, approximately 200,000 immigrants entered Canada. For the last half century, Canada's immigrant population has remained fairly constant, at 15% to 17% of the total population.

Highway 400, Ontario,
1959.
Photo by Kryn Taconis,
courtesy National Archives
of Canada, PA-169942.

Sonic Boomers

The birth rate of a country tends to rise and fall in tandem with its economic well-being and sense of optimism. Certainly, in the Canada of the 1930s, the birth rate fell dramatically and recovered only marginally during the war. By the 1950s, Canadians seemed to feel a great urge to nest and were supported in this desire by a booming economy.

It has been estimated that, in any given year during the late 1940s and early 1950s, about 20% of women in their twenties were giving birth. From 1940 to 1959, the number of births per year in Canada rose from 253,000 to nearly 480,000. For statisticians, this has indeed been the sonic boom of Canadian demographic trends.

Not surprisingly, the baby boom has had, and continues to have, a huge impact on Canadian society. Hospital maternity wards were the first to feel the pinch and struggled to cope; then there was a run on everything from diapers to baby food to children's clothing. By the 1950s, the boomers were ready for school and so enrolments doubled. By the 1960s, many boomers were on to college or to university and expenditures on education rose from just under $439 million in 1950 to about $7.6 billion in 1970. In the 1970s, boomers vied for entry-level jobs in the labour force.

Unlike their parents, however, the boomers have tended to have smaller families. They have had less formal, and some have said less stable, marriages. They have also been more prepared than their parents to raise children alone, without the benefit of a resident spouse.

Montréal, Quebec, 1957.
Photo by Marcel Cognac,
courtesy Canadian Museum
of Contemporary
Photography.

John Harris, Katy Harris-
Mcleod, Creemore, Ontario.
Photo by Pamela Harris.

"But I know these things

only because older people told me . . .

All I had to do was listen —

When their day's work was done

they gathered on street corners and

traded stories long into the night . . .

[they] were superb storytellers,

practitioners of an art they

didn't learn from books — and the

best of them were always the oldest."

Bill McNeil, from *Voice of the Pioneer*, Fitzhenry and Whiteside

As they age, into the 2000s and 2010s, boomers will impact on the market for retirement saving plans, senior-oriented housing, and vacation and leisure packages. Ultimately, they will heavily influence the need for pension plans, senior health care and even funeral services.

The boomers are the most numerous segment of society: just over one-quarter of Canada's population is boomer born. Their birth dates fall anywhere between 1946 and 1966, and as the century closes they thus find themselves aged anywhere from 33 to 53 years.

An Aging Population

Statisticians tell us that, by 2016, some 16% of our expected 37 million people will be elderly. In 1900, by comparison, just 5% of the population was elderly and in mid-century, slightly less than 8%. Today, some 12% of our population is 65 and older. The increase in the proportion of seniors is partly due to low fertility, and the fact that there are relatively fewer children.

Canadians are also living longer. In 1931, life expectancy at birth was 60 years for men and 62 years for women. In the 1950s, life expectancy rose to 66 for men and 71 for women. Today, it stands at about 76 years for men and 81 years for women.

The difference in life expectancy for men and women means men will most likely die with a spouse at their sides. For example, of the population aged 75 and over, almost 63% are women and of the population aged 90 and over, 76% are women. A Canadian woman has a higher probability than her male counterpart of nursing an ailing spouse and then living alone once her spouse has passed on.

Traditionally, older widows in Canada lived with either a sibling or with the family of a son or daughter. We know that in 1971, for example, 26% of women without a spouse, and aged 75 and older, lived in the home of another. A further 26% lived alone. But in 1991, those living with another had fallen to 12% and those living alone had risen to 39%. There are differing views about this. One is that families, caught in the time crunch, may not have as much time for Granny anymore. The other is that families double up when there are housing shortages, but prefer their own space when such space is available and affordable. Nevertheless, close to one in six adult Canadians provides at least one hour a week to helping seniors.

I SPENT EIGHT YEARS OF MY LIFE IN THE UNITED STATES RIGHT AROUND THE TIME OF SPUTNIK. IT WAS REALLY THE GLORY TIME FOR SCIENCE WHEN THE AMERICANS WERE TRYING TO CATCH UP WITH THE RUSSIANS. WHEN I WAS READY — I HAD A PhD AND ALL THAT — THERE WERE JOBS FOR THE TAKING IN THE UNITED STATES BUT I TURNED THEM DOWN AND WENT BACK TO CANADA.

CANADA WAS QUEBEC. IT WAS MEDICARE, TOMMY DOUGLAS AND THE NATIONAL FILM BOARD. IT WAS THE CBC. THESE WERE THE THINGS THAT DREW ME BACK.

YES, I HAD BEEN INTERNED DURING THE WAR WITH MY PARENTS, AND THAT WAS A TERRIBLE THING, BUT OUT OF IT CAME MULRONEY'S REPARATIONS. CANADA IS COMMITTED TO ITS OWN. CANADA IS MY HOME.

David Suzuki, broadcaster and journalist

Front yard, Bavarian Village,

Robert Wanka, 1989.

Photo by Brenda Pelkey.

THE SOCIETY

The Canadian historian Desmond Morton once wrote: "History tells Canadians only that they live in a tough old country, that they have a tradition of compromise, an aversion to violence, and a gift for survival. Only Switzerland and the United States have older federal systems, and both of them have survived cruel civil wars." Northrop Frye, the well-known Canadian literary critic, was convinced that "the Canadian genius for compromise is reflected in the existence of Canada itself."

Certainly, the Fathers of Confederation were deeply mindful of this genius for compromise when they set out to unite the country. They knew well that the citizens of the new nation spoke two of the major languages of the world, belonged to different religious denominations and had differing legal systems. They saw clearly that the regions of this great land were widely dispersed and unequal in wealth and population. A single government, they realized, could never accommodate these realities, nor would the provinces submit to such a plan.

Thus, Canada came together as a confederation. Today, its powers are distributed between the federal government and the governments of the provinces and territories. This sharing ensures that the unique cultural, linguistic, legal and economic realities of our land are respected within a national framework. For example, among the powers assigned to the provinces at Confederation were the socially and culturally sensitive matters of education, health and the administration of justice.

Yet, when the Dominion of Canada came into being in 1867, its governments were simple and rudimentary affairs. Canada's federal government employed only 1,500 people. This small staff worked largely at maintaining bridges and roads and at keeping the mails moving. Indeed, by 1871, the federal government was able to carry out all these duties with revenues of just $5.50 per Canadian, about the cost of a year's newspaper subscription at the time.

By the turn of the century, schools, hospitals, and even the justice system were just emerging as formations of a fledgling state. Social services, on the other hand, came from private charities and religious institutions, as well as one's own family and neighbours. The truly major expenses of the day were for canals and railways.

Some 130 years later, more than 2 million people run Canada's governments—federal, provincial, territorial and local—as well as the education, health and justice sectors. As the 20th century draws to a close, all governments collectively spend more than $390 billion a year. In 1996, federal taxes for a Canadian family earning between $40,000 and $60,000 came to about $6,975.

The growth of government in Canada has been fuelled by the state's expanding role in health, education and welfare: in fact, increased spending in these sectors alone has been responsible for more than half the total growth in government expenditures since the end of the Second World War. Today, education and health account for about 50% of provincial and territorial spending.

At the federal level, the major expense is for "transfer payments to persons," which in 1998 totalled $54.5 billion. These transfer payments refer to the major income-security programs such as Old Age Security, Employment Insurance, and veterans' pensions. This expense is followed by payments toward the public debt, which totalled $42.5 billion. Direct taxes from individual Canadians constitute the largest single source of revenue for the federal government—in 1998, taxes amounted to $81 billion.

The chief order of business for most Canadian governments in the last decade of the 20th century has been to restrain spending and control deficits. To this end, work forces have been reduced, and in 1998, there were almost 365,000 fewer public sector employees than there were in 1992. Governments have accomplished the downsizing not only by cutting staff, but by reducing budgets, privatizing public assets and contracting services previously produced in-house.

By 1997–98, through such cost-reduction efforts and an accompanying growth in revenue, federal, provincial and territorial governments had moved from a record deficit ($66 billion in 1992–93) to a surplus of $3.5 billion, the first to be recorded in 28 years.

Having successfully brought down the deficit, the public sector experienced a new-found fiscal freedom and began hiring again. In 1998, the number of public sector workers expanded for the first time in four years, with the addition of some 35,000 people, largely in the health, social services and education sectors.

Indeed, two important indications of a well-governed nation are the health and education of its people. Canadians have among the longest life expectancies in the world and are also very well educated: about

40% of the population 15 years of age and older today has graduated from college or university.

Yet, as a result of government curbs on spending, there have been some dramatic changes in the health, education and justice systems. For example, in 1975, there were 206 police officers for every 100,000 Canadians. By 1997, there were 181.

In the health sector, hospitals and hospital beds have been shut down, and $3 of every $10 spent on health care now comes directly from the pockets of individual Canadians and their private insurers rather than from governments. Since 1980, tuition for a full-time undergraduate arts student has risen 115%. For the 1998–99 academic year, that would have meant, on average, fees of just over $3,100.

Unfortunately, all Canadians do not share equally in the country's social achievements. Poverty, poor education, low social status and unstable employment still thwart progress for many. Young people who haven't completed high school are seriously disadvantaged in the job market: between 1981 and 1996, their unemployment rate climbed from 10% to 18%.

Today, the poorest Canadian can expect to die on average four years before the wealthiest. Canadians with less than a Grade 9 education and those with a history of unemployment are greatly overrepresented in our prisons.

The Law

There's an apparent riddle when it comes to law and order in Canada. The polls tell us that many Canadians, especially those 55 years and older, are worried about rising levels of

Evacuation of the
Unemployed Office Workers,
1985.
Work by Eleanor Bond, from
Work Station.

crime. The surveys tell us that crime rates are actually falling; in 1997, for instance, the crime rate was the lowest it had been since 1980.

The solution to the riddle is quite simple: the 1997 crime rate was still 120% higher than it was 30 years earlier.

From 1966 to 1975, the incidence of homicides, the most serious and widely feared of crimes, increased by 142%. In 1966, this meant that 1 out of every 100,000 Canadians would die as the result of a homicide. By 1975, this had climbed to more than 3 out of every 100,000 Canadians. Then, a powerful reversal set in as the incidence of killings began to fall. By 1997, Canada's murder rate had come down to 1.92 for every 100,000 people.

It's difficult to pin down what has caused these roller-coaster crime rate variations. Some police forces, for example, give credit for falling crime rates to recent improvements in community-based policing and intensified efforts to prevent crime.

However, there are still ups and downs in the crime rates and these may be due to changes in society's view of what constitutes a crime, newly outlawed offences, a shift in the willingness of citizens to report incidents or a change in police enforcement practices.

One thing is certain: in Canada, we are older and the population 55 years and older is simply less likely to engage in crime. Undoubtedly for similar reasons, homicides have fallen in the United States, France, Italy and Germany. Although Canada's murder rate is about three to four times lower than that of the United States, it is higher than rates in many European countries, including England,

where the rate is only 1 person per 100,000. Killings all too often bespeak a deadly intimacy. The fate of more than half of all Canadian homicide victims is to die in their own homes at the hands of someone they know. In 1997, only 13% of all victims were killed by strangers. More than half of all adult women killed are murdered by someone with whom they have, or once had, an intimate relationship.

While the overall crime rate in Canada has fallen, between 1987 and 1997 there was a 119% increase in the rate of Canadians aged 12 to 17 charged with common assault. Such assaults, which involve incidents of pushing, slapping, punching, or face-to-face verbal threats (but not weapons), are regarded with little tolerance in Canadian schools as a consequence of current practices referred to as "zero tolerance."

As a whole, youth crime in Canada has declined since 1991. The great majority of youth offences today (1997) are still non-violent, and when young people do commit a crime, it's most likely to be a theft or a break and enter. These two categories account for 43% of all youths charged.

Victims of youth violence bear a strong resemblance to their persecutors. Young people tend, quite simply, to target other young people. Young males are the most likely to be victims of crime—they account for 36% of all crime victims. Older Canadians, despite their concerns, seldom fall victim to criminals.

In 1999, the federal government introduced a new Youth Criminal Justice Act in the House of Commons to replace the Young Offenders Act. The new Act is intended to better distinguish between violent and non-violent

Courtesy Canada Post
Corporation.

crime and to strengthen efforts to rehabilitate young people who have committed crimes.

Scales of Justice The Canadian justice system employs two kinds of law. Common law, used in all provinces except Quebec, is based on principles developed in medieval England and relies on court judgments as precedents.

The civil law of Quebec dates back even farther, to the Roman Empire, and reflects many precepts of French law: in it, judges look first to a written code (the *code civil*) for guidance and then to precedents set by earlier decisions. In practice, the decisions arrived at by these two legal systems are often much the same.

In 1994–95, governments spent nearly $10 billion on the justice system, or $340 for every man, woman and child in Canada. Within the justice system, policing expenditures are the biggest single item. In 1997, they totalled almost $6 billion, or about $200 for each Canadian. Overall, Canadian governments spend about one-quarter as much on justice as they do on health.

In Canada, each province is responsible for establishing its own courts, which deal with matters arising under both federal and provincial law. The Parliament of Canada has created a number of federal courts, including the Supreme Court of Canada, the highest court of the land. Since the Canadian Charter of Rights and Freedoms became part of the Constitution in 1982, the Supreme Court has had increased responsibilities. From 1982 through 1998, it heard some 400 Charter-related cases.

Canada's Police In 1870, when Canada negotiated the acquisition of the vast territories of the West from the Hudson's Bay Company, there was no major police force in Canada. Even the largest cities, Montréal and Toronto, had few full-time constables, and small towns and rural communities were without a police force altogether. To remedy this, the Canadian government created a temporary police force that would administer the Western lands peacefully and hopefully avert the kind of warfare that settlers and Aboriginal peoples had experienced in the western United States.

In August 1873, an advance guard of what became our national police force, the Royal Canadian Mounted Police (RCMP), was sent to winter in Fort Garry in Manitoba.

Today, in addition to enforcing federal statutes, the RCMP is the sole law enforcement body in Canada's territories and is employed by 8 of the 10 provinces to carry out provincial policing responsibilities.

Ontario and Quebec have their own police forces—the Ontario Provincial Police and the Sûrété du Québec. The Royal Newfoundland Constabulary, which is the provincial police force of Newfoundland, patrols the province's three largest municipalities, St. John's, Corner Brook, and Labrador City, as well as Churchill Falls. The RCMP polices the rest of the province.

Canada's police officers are highly regarded by Canadians. In an international survey of 11 western industrialized countries in 1996, Canada had the highest percentage of the public (80%) who believe their police are effective in controlling crime—despite having the third lowest number of officers per 100,000 of the population.

The public's faith seems well placed: each

"They always get their man."

year, Canadian police solve more than three-quarters of all reported homicides. Approximately two-thirds of all cases heard in the youth and adult courts of Canada result in convictions.

The current rate of imprisonment in Canada is 115 people per 100,000. This is far below the rate in the United States, with its 600 incarcerated for every 100,000, but it greatly exceeds the rate in many other countries, including Japan (37), Sweden (65) and Germany (85).

In 1996, Canada's adult jails held some 37,000 prisoners. Each adult inmate cost the taxpayer about $44,000 a year. Aboriginal Canadians accounted for 17% of all adult prisoners, although they made up only 2% of the adult population.

Overwhelmingly, Canada's adult inmates are men (95% in 1996), and they are younger and more likely to have been unemployed than the average adult. They are also much less educated: while only 19% of Canadian adults did not go beyond Grade 9 in school, 36% of the inmates in our jails have a Grade 9 education or less.

Education in Canada

In Quebec, in the mid-17th century, nuns from religious orders like the Ursulines and the Congregation of Notre Dame provided elementary instruction in catechism, reading, writing and arithmetic. Often these Sisters were itinerant teachers, travelling through the countryside to offer schooling.

In the early 19th century, many Canadian women, though not trained as educators, opened their homes to welcome young children for instruction. These early centres of learning were known as the "dame" schools. One-room schoolhouses, or *petites écoles* as they were called in French Canada, were common in frontier settlements well into the 20th century.

In the years following Confederation, education was still a limited and precious resource. At the first Census, in 1871, fully a fifth of those in their twenties and older could neither read nor write. As recently as 1951, half of all adults in Canada had not completed Grade 9.

Over the span of the 20th century, an extensive system of schools has evolved. In 1995–96, there were nearly 16,000 elementary and secondary schools in Canada. Today, some 200 community colleges and related institutions complement Canada's approximately 75 universities.

As the 20th century closes, Canada ranks among the world leaders in educational attainment. Over a lifetime, a Canadian can expect to spend more than three years in a postsecondary institution, a figure exceeded only by Australia among the 29 members of the Organisation for Economic Co-operation and Development (OECD).

Indeed, Canada is one of the few countries in the world today where more women than men graduate from college and university. Young women in their twenties have so outpaced their male counterparts as graduates that by 1996, 51% of these women had a degree or diploma, compared with 42% of the men.

"Well, you're young. You know a whole lot you won't know later on."

Margaret Laurence, *The Diviners*

Canadian men in the 30-to-44 age group who have graduated from university earn on average up to 50% more than those with high school graduation only. But for Canadian women of the same age, the financial rewards are even greater: those who graduate from university can expect to earn up to 80% more than female secondary graduates.

The Cost Among the OECD countries, Canada and Denmark spend the largest percentage of their national income on education—between 7% and 8% annually. In 1995, Canada devoted 7.6% of its gross domestic product (GDP) to this sector. On a per student basis, Canada is tied with four other OECD countries for top place in expenditures on postsecondary education: Australia, Sweden, Switzerland and the United States.

In 1998–99, education expenditures in Canada totalled more than $60 billion. Of this amount, almost $38 billion went to elementary and secondary schools, with their enrolment of 5.7 million students. With some 830,000 full- and part-time university students and over a half million in community colleges, Quebec CÉGEPs *(Collèges d'enseignement général et professionnel)* and similar institutions, the cost of postsecondary education came to about $16.5 billion.

Canada is unique among industrialized nations in having no federal department of education. The provinces and territories are responsible for this sector and are its primary source of funding. In 1998–99, they supplied an estimated $37 billion for education at all levels. At the postsecondary level, however, students, not government, pay a greater portion of the costs of their education.

From 1980 to 1997, tuition costs spiralled upwards, growing 115%, while average family income rose only 1% (after adjusting for inflation). Not surprisingly, paying off student loans is now a major preoccupation for young Canadians. For every $100 owed by a graduate in 1982, a graduate of 1995 owed about $240.

Despite these costs, Canadians continue to flock to university and college. They have eminently good reasons to do so, both intellectually and economically. In 1995, some 23% of young male high school graduates with no postsecondary education worked as security guards, janitors and kitchen helpers. A full 45% of those with a high school education were employed in jobs that did not require even a high school diploma.

One consequence of this has been what educators call the "time-outs" or "stop-outs"— young Canadians who, having dropped out of school, eventually return to finish their studies. In 1991, for example, about 18% of 20-year-olds had left high school without graduating. Four years later, so many of them had returned that the true drop-out rate was down to 15%.

(Right)
Ottawa Ladies' College
group, 1909.
Courtesy National Archives
of Canada, PA-042397.

(Below)
Molson School, Manitoba.
Courtesy National Archives
of Canada, C-047077.

(Middle right)
School train, Chapleau,
Ontario.
Courtesy National Archives
of Canada, PA-142372.

(Bottom right)
School for disabled children.
Courtesy National Archives
of Canada, C-034841.

Alberni Indian Residential
School, Port Alberni,
British Columbia, c. 1906.
Courtesy Alberni Valley
Museum Collection,
PN3259.

SEVENTH GENERATION The award-winning Native playwright and novelist Tomson Highway has said of the future of Canada's Indigenous peoples: "The shamans who predicted the arrival of the white man and the near destruction of the Indian people also foretold the resurgence of the Native people seven lifetimes after Columbus. We are that seventh generation."

On the other hand, the health status of Aboriginal people in Canada has been described as "both a tragedy and a crisis." In 1996, the Royal Commission on Aboriginal Peoples told Canadians that registered Indians have a life expectancy seven to eight years shorter than that of other Canadians; that Aboriginal infant mortality is twice the national average of 6.1 per 1,000 live births; and that infectious diseases occur in higher rates among Aboriginal people than among other Canadians. The suicide rate of those aged 15 to 24 is five to eight times the national average.

Certainly, Canada's Aboriginal peoples have been making progress in land claims and self-governance. In 1993, the Canadian government and Canada's Inuit reached an important agreement regarding land settlement and Aboriginal rights. As a result, Nunavut was carved out of the Northwest Territories in 1999. This new territory covers an area more than three-and-a-half times the size of France, with a population of 26,500.

In 1996, Canada's Aboriginal identity population was approximately 800,000, or about 3% of the total population. One-third were North American Indians

(554,000) and one-quarter were Métis (210,000), while Inuit (41,000) comprised 1 in 20 of the total Aboriginal population.

Because of higher fertility rates, Canada's Aboriginal population is growing more rapidly than the population in general. In Winnipeg, Regina and Saskatoon, about 12% of those under age 15 are Aboriginal. One-third of all Aboriginal children under the age of 15 live in lone-parent families, twice the rate of the general population.

About one in four of Canada's Aboriginal people learned an Aboriginal mother tongue, but only one in seven speaks an Aboriginal language at home. Of all the Native languages, Cree is the mother tongue of the largest proportion of Aboriginal people (10.0%), followed by Inuktitut (3.4%) and Ojibway (2.8%). English is the mother tongue for the majority of the Aboriginal population (68%) while French is the mother tongue for only 6%. Of all the provinces, Quebec has the highest proportion of Aboriginal people—almost half, compared with about one in six in Ontario—who speak a Native language as mother tongue.

Out of all Aboriginal people in Canada, four out of five live west of Quebec and more than half live in urban areas.

At the beginning of this decade, 6 out of 10 Canadians over age 15 had jobs, whereas in the Aboriginal community only 4 out of 10 were employed. In 1996, while Aboriginal people accounted for about 2% of the overall adult population, they represented 17% of all prison inmates.

Arms of Nunavut.

Flag of Nunavut.

NUNAVUT If the new territory of Nunavut (created April 1, 1999) were placed over Europe, it would stretch from Oslo, Norway, all the way down to Africa, as far as Libya. Carved out of the eastern and central section of Canada's vast Northwest Territories, Nunavut covers an area of some 2 million km², but for all its space, the territory has just 26,500 inhabitants and 21 km of paved roads.

Nunavut, which means "our land" in Inuktitut, is the result of the largest Aboriginal land claim in Canadian history and for the Eastern Arctic Inuit, the culmination of a long-time dream of self-government. The capital, Iqaluit, on the south shore of Baffin Island, is the largest settlement, with 4,200 inhabitants. Its northernmost community is Grise Fiord, located at 77° north latitude.

Although sparse, Nunavut's population grew by nearly 19% between 1991 and 1998—more than twice the national average. About 83% Inuit, this is a population of larger families: the average holds 4.1 persons compared with 3.1 for the whole of Canada. Nunavut is younger, on average, than the rest of Canada: fully 40% of its population is 15 and under, compared with 21% nationally.

Residents of Nunavut face higher unemployment, lower incomes and a higher cost of living than do other Canadians. In 1996, family incomes averaged $48,866 a year here compared with $54,583 nationally. The cost of living in Iqaluit is about 65% higher than in Montréal. For example, two litres of milk here can cost about $7 and a loaf of bread, $3.

The birth of Nunavut transforms the map of Canada for the first time since Newfoundland joined Canada 50 years ago. The territory's legislative assembly has 19 members.

ELIZABETH THE SECOND

By the grace of God of the United Kingdom, Canada and her other Realms and Territories Queen, Head of the Commonwealth, Defender of the Faith.

To all to whom these Presents shall come or whom the same may in anyway concern —

GREETING:

A PROCLAMATION

Attorney General of Canada

WHEREAS in the past certain amendments to the Constitution of Canada have been made by the Parliament of the United Kingdom at the request and with the consent of Canada;

AND WHEREAS it is in accord with the status of Canada as an independent state that Canadians be able to amend their Constitution in Canada in all respects;

AND WHEREAS it is desirable to provide in the Constitution of Canada for the recognition of certain fundamental rights and freedoms and to make other amendments to the Constitution;

AND WHEREAS the Parliament of the United Kingdom has therefore, at the request and with the consent of Canada, enacted the Canada Act, which provides for the patriation and amendment of the Constitution of Canada;

AND WHEREAS section 58 of the Constitution Act, 1982, set out in Schedule B to the Canada Act, provides that the Constitution Act, 1982 shall, subject to section 59 thereof, come into force on a day to be fixed by proclamation issued under the Great Seal of Canada;

NOW KNOW You that We, by and with the advice of Our Privy Council for Canada, do by this Our Proclamation, declare that the Constitution Act, 1982 shall, subject to section 59 thereof, come into force on the Seventeenth day of April, in the Year of Our Lord One Thousand Nine Hundred and Eighty-two.

OF ALL WHICH Our Loving Subjects and all others whom these Presents may concern are hereby required to take notice and to govern themselves accordingly.

IN TESTIMONY WHEREOF We have caused these Our Letters to be made Patent and the Great Seal of Canada to be hereunto affixed.

At Our City of Ottawa, this Seventeenth day of April in the Year of Our Lord One Thousand Nine Hundred and Eighty-two and in the Thirty-first Year of Our Reign.

By Her Majesty's Command

Registrar General of Canada

Prime Minister of Canada

GOD SAVE THE QUEEN

ELIZABETH DEUX

Par la grâce de Dieu Reine du Royaume-Uni, du Canada et de ses autres Royaumes et Territoires, Chef du Commonwealth, Défenseur de la Foi.

À tous ceux que les présentes peuvent de quelque manière concerner.

SALUT:

PROCLAMATION

Le procureur général du Canada

CONSIDÉRANT:

Qu'à la demande et avec le consentement du Canada, le Parlement du Royaume-Uni a déjà modifié à plusieurs reprises la Constitution du Canada;

Qu'en vertu de leur appartenance à un État souverain, les Canadiens se doivent de détenir tout pouvoir de modifier leur Constitution au Canada;

Qu'il est souhaitable d'inscrire dans la Constitution du Canada la reconnaissance d'un certain nombre de libertés et de droits fondamentaux et d'y apporter d'autres modifications;

Que le Parlement du Royaume-Uni, à la demande et avec le consentement du Canada, a adopté en conséquence la Loi sur le Canada, qui prévoit le rapatriement de la Constitution canadienne et sa modification;

Que l'article 58, figurant à l'annexe B de la Loi sur le Canada, stipule que, sous réserve de l'article 59, la Loi constitutionnelle de 1982 entrera en vigueur à une date fixée par proclamation sous le grand sceau du Canada,

NOUS PROCLAMONS, sur l'avis de Notre Conseil privé pour le Canada, que la Loi constitutionnelle de 1982 entrera en vigueur, sous réserve de l'article 59, le dix-septième jour du mois d'avril en l'an de grâce mil neuf cent quatre-vingt-deux.

NOUS DEMANDONS À Nos loyaux sujets et à toute autre personne concernée de prendre acte de la présente proclamation.

EN FOI DE QUOI, Nous avons rendu les présentes lettres patentes et y avons fait apposer le grand sceau du Canada.

Fait en Notre ville d'Ottawa, ce dix-septième jour du mois d'avril en l'an de grâce mil neuf cent quatre-vingt-deux, le trente et unième de Notre règne.

Par ordre de Sa Majesté

Le registraire général du Canada

Le premier ministre du Canada

DIEU PROTÈGE LA REINE

NOTE ON THE VOTE The right to vote is one of the most basic rights of a citizen. But at Confederation, in 1867, it belonged to just 11% of the population and almost all were males who owned property. In 1915, May Clendenan, a Western Canadian advocate of women's rights, expressed the following sentiment on the issue of the vote: "If democracy is right, women should have it. If it isn't, men shouldn't."

The first province to allow women the vote was Manitoba, in 1916. Two years later, in 1918, all Canadian women aged 21 or older won the right to vote in federal elections. Most Canadians of Asian ancestry were denied the vote in the 19th and early 20th centuries. It was only in 1948 that Japanese Canadians were given the franchise. Non-Status Indians received full voting rights provincially between 1949 and 1969, and the federal vote was extended to the Inuit in 1950, and to Status Indians in 1960.

Today, with a few exceptions such as senior electoral officials, all Canadian citizens aged 18 and older can vote. This right is guaranteed in the 1982 Canadian Charter of Rights and Freedoms.

"The spirit walking

in the sky

takes care of me."

Ojibwa song

Canada's Health

In 1954, Tommy Douglas, then premier of Saskatchewan and about to be the "father" of Canadian medicare, said, "I made a pledge that if I ever had anything to do with it, people would be able to get health services just as they are able to get educational services, as an inalienable right of being a citizen."

At that time, people like Tommy Douglas still had vivid memories of the Great Depression, when many Canadians could not pay their medical bills and the indigent flooded the hospitals, while bankrupt municipalities, especially on the Prairies, could do almost nothing to help.

Out of such memories came Douglas' steely resolve to establish public health care insurance in Canada. Saskatchewan was the first province to insure both hospital and physician care. Since the early 1970s, all the provinces and territories have provided permanent residents of Canada with comprehensive coverage for all medically necessary hospital and physician services.

Today, the Canada Health Act, which governs federal contributions to the provinces, requires that provincial plans meet five standards: they must be available to all permanent residents and provide comprehensive services; they must also be equally accessible to all the insured, be portable to other provinces, and be publicly administered. While health insurance in Canada is publicly funded, the Canadian system is not "socialized medicine." Canadians are free to choose their own doctors, who are usually in private or group practice and independent of government.

Remembrance Day,
St. John's, Newfoundland.
Photo by Barbara Shenstone.

"For Sale — One Home-Made Coffin.

Never been Used. Fit 6'2".

Reason for Selling: Improved Health.

Phone 97937."

Classified ad, *Saskatoon Star Phoenix*, 1945

Most of today's Canadians claim they enjoy a sense of physical well-being. Typically, we spend about 90% of our lives free of disabling health problems. Trends over the last decade confirm many improvements: lower rates of death from heart disease and strokes for both men and women, and from cancer in males. Infant mortality has fallen 60% in a generation, and accidental deaths have declined substantially in the past 25 years.

Yet every era finds its own diseases and disabilities. Until the 20th century, patients in Canadian hospitals who were suffering from infectious and nutritional diseases like tuberculosis, pneumonia and scurvy tended to be very poor. Since then, many conditions that were once a deep concern to Canadians have all but disappeared. Diphtheria, for example, is now a scourge of the past. In 1953, polio was such a severe health problem, it struck almost 60 of every 100,000 Canadians. With the arrival of the Salk vaccine in 1955, there were few new cases of this disease in Canada.

One consequence of our improved health is our longevity. A Canadian male born in the 1990s can expect to live 75.7 years—a female, 81.4 years. In the late 1800s, the dismal reality was that men could expect to live only about 42 years, and women only about 45, while one out of four people died before reaching a 10th birthday.

Health Culprits Cancers of all kinds are the leading cause of death in Canada: in 1996, they were responsible for more than 28% of male deaths and 27% of female deaths. Close behind is the second biggest killer, heart disease, which accounted for nearly 22% of male deaths and 19% of female deaths. Strokes are the third largest cause of death.

Because the Canadian population is aging, deaths from cancer and new cancer cases are growing. In 1998, there were nearly 130,000 new cases and 63,000 deaths from cancer. The most encouraging development, however, is the steady decline in cancer mortality since 1969 among men and women under 60 years of age.

Among Canadian adults, musculoskeletal disorders, especially non-arthritic back problems, arthritis and rheumatism, are a major cause of disability, pain and visits to the doctor. While today's children are generally healthy, one of every three has a chronic condition. Some 20% are afflicted with allergies and 11% with asthma. Asthma is being diagnosed in more children than previously: in 1978, only 2.5% of children under 15 years were reported as having the condition, but by 1994, that number had risen to over 11%.

Health and Poverty Good health is not shared equally. On average, the wealthy are in better health than the middle class, who in turn are healthier than the poor. The well educated are healthier than the less educated; the employed are healthier than the unemployed. Poverty, unemployment and poor education all limit the health choices and the health of Canadians. Children who live in low-income households are more likely to have health problems than those in higher income families. Just as education and income are related, higher levels of both are linked to better health and well-being.

Canadians living in poverty suffer higher rates of such chronic diseases as high blood pressure, emphysema and stomach ulcers than others. Low income is also a predictor of premature death. Even after factors like gender, smoking and chronic diseases are taken into account, low-income Canadians under age 75 are twice as likely to die in the next two years as those in middle- and high-income groups.

The latest international comparisons on health care costs show that Canada spent 9.2% of its GDP on health in 1996. Only four other OECD countries exceeded this, first and foremost the United States, which spent 13.6% of its GDP on health in the same year.

In 1998, health care expenditures in Canada totalled $80 billion, an increase of 3.8% over 1997. This came to $2,613 for every Canadian, the highest per capita amount in our history. The total represented 9.1% of our GDP, a slight decline from 1996 but a significant drop from the 10.0% we spent in 1992.

The balance between public and private funding has shifted in recent times. In 1975, for example, Canadians and their private insurers paid less than 24% of the total health care bill. By 1998, some 30% of all spending on health care came from private sources, with the remaining 70% provided by governments.

In the health care system, hospitals are the largest single expense. In 1998, they cost about $27 billion, or roughly one-third of all health spending, while physician services, followed closely by drugs, are the next most expensive items, accounting for about 14.5% and 14.0% respectively of the total.

Government in Canada

In the 1850s, when Queen Victoria was considering which of five Canadian cities—Montréal, Toronto, Kingston, Québec, or Ottawa—to select as the permanent capital, she received some secret advice from the then Governor General, Sir Edmund Head. "Choose Ottawa," he suggested. It's "the least objectionable" choice. As "every city is jealous of every other except Ottawa, Ottawa will be the favourite second choice of all."

Differences and disagreements between the governments of Canada—federal, provincial, territorial and local—are said to be as quintessentially Canadian as maple syrup or Arctic char, as inevitable as winter in Manitoba. Since the birth of the country, the

René Lévesque, sometime
in the 1960s.
Photo by Ted Grant.

tone of government has been characterized by conflict and compromise. Nonetheless, the structure of the Canadian confederation has also been capable of change and evolution.

Many of the powers assigned to the provinces in 1867, including education, health and the administration of justice, seemed of negligible importance. As the state became more active in these spheres, the influence and scope of provincial and local governments increased. From 1926 to the mid-1990s, total expenditures by all governments rose from 16% to 50% of the GDP. In that time, provincial government expenditures, excluding intergovernmental transfers, rose from 3% to 17%.

Constitutional Issues In the last few decades, the potential separation of Quebec from Canada has occupied centre stage in the national psyche. The Parti Québécois, which forms the province's government and is devoted to Quebec sovereignty, was re-elected in November of 1998.

Since the late 1980s, Canadian governments have undertaken two major but unsuccessful efforts at formal constitutional reform: the Meech Lake Accord of 1987 (which would have brought Quebec into the Constitution) and the Charlottetown Accord of 1991–92 (which would have recognized Quebec as a distinct society but was rejected by Canadians in a national referendum).

In 1996, Parliament passed a resolution recognizing Quebec as a distinct society. It also guaranteed Canada's five major regions that no constitutional change concerning them would be made without their unanimous consent. The provinces are gaining more power: the federal government has been transferring greater responsibility for some programs, including labour-market training and mining and forestry development, to the provinces.

The current federal government is formed by the Liberal Party of Canada. It was elected in the last federal election, in 1997, when 67% of eligible voters cast a ballot. The Reform Party of Canada placed second, thus becoming the official Opposition. The other parties in the House of Commons are the Bloc Québécois, the New Democratic Party of Canada, and the Progressive Conservative Party of Canada. One Independent was also elected.

In the 1999 federal budget, the Government of Canada announced that its books would once again be balanced when fiscal 1998–99 came to a close. With its improved finances, the government committed itself to investing an additional $11.5 billion over the next five years in cash transfers to the provinces for health care, and to increasing federal funding for health research. The budget also introduced personal income tax reductions for all Canadian taxpayers. The tax relief measures in the budget were projected to amount to $16.5 billion over a three-year period.

(Right)

Prime Minister

Jean Chrétien, 1998.

Photo by J.M. Carisse,

Office of the Prime Minister.

THE OTTAWA EVENING CITIZEN

Page One —— Ottawa, Canada, Tuesday, May 16, 1939. —— Section E

The Royal Visit to Canada---Souvenir Number

Princess Elizabeth's Natural Talents Now Being Developed Rapidly

Interests Are Developing in Normal Way

There Is No Danger That the "Girl" Will Be Lost in the "Princess." Her Favorite Study Subjects.

WHEN the girl who was to become Queen Victoria first realized the dignity and responsibility to which she was heir, she uttered the famous comment: "I will be good."

The rather touching solemnity of this remark forms a sharp contrast with Princess Elizabeth's response when, in her turn, she learnt that she might be Queen of England:

"If ever I am Queen, the first thing I shall do will be to make a law forbidding people to ride or drive on Sunday. Horses MUST have a holiday!"

These words show rather more than a practical good sense and a fondness for horses — both of which are characteristic of the Princess. They indicate that, unlike so many children destined to wear a crown, she has had a childhood in the true sense.

In bringing up her daughters, Queen Elizabeth has consistently allowed them to enjoy family life and the ordinary routine of lessons and games followed by girls who are not princesses, introducing them gradually to the formality and responsibility of their position.

At the age of 13, Princess Elizabeth is becoming more conscious of the formal side of her life, and sometimes kindly but firmly represses the exuberance of her younger sister, Princess Margaret, if the latter fails to reach what she regards as the necessary standard of decorum in their public appearances together.

Developing Naturally.

But this increasing self-consciousness is developing naturally, and there is no danger that the girl will be lost in the princess. Her interests are the normal interests of an intelligent and active girl—although perhaps her particular fondness for grammar is rather an unusual taste. Latin and mythology are her other favorite subjects from a curriculum, which includes scripture, French, arithmetic, geometry, geography, literature and history.

Special attention is paid to constitutional history, and Lady Cynthia Asquith, the author of a biography of King George VI's daughters, writes that "Princess Elizabeth is under no illusion that modern monarchies can be safeguarded by any pretensions to 'Divine Right,' the appeal to tradition, or the exercise of force. She knows they can be justified and preserved only by the highest form of public service by understanding and sympathy, and the most diligent devotion to the general welfare."

Music, dancing and drawing—in all of which she is proficient without showing any outstanding talent—form part of Princess Elizabeth's regular studies. She is a good natural dancer, but in music she will probably be excelled by her younger sister, who, at the age of 11 months, startled her grandmother, Lady Strathmore, by distinctly humming the "Merry Widow" waltz.

Riding and swimming are Princess Elizabeth's favorite sports. She has been awarded a swimming medal by the Bath Club, to which she and her sister go regularly when in London. Gymnastics, orthodox and unorthodox, also appeal to her.

"I have watched her," writes Lady Cynthia, "bounding like a young stag over a rope held at a height which several contemporaries—some of them boys—shamefacedly but firmly declined to attempt."

Books She Reads.

In the books they read and the games they play, the two Princesses share the same tastes as many thousands of other English girls. A list of "books read" kept by Princess Elizabeth shows such titles as "Alice in Wonderland," "Stories from the Odyssey," and "The Wind in the Willows."

She likes to choose her own books, and once when a church dignitary offered to send her a book as a memento of his visit to Glamis Castle (the home of the Queen's parents, Lord and Lady Strathmore), she said: "Oh, thank you! It would be kind of you to send me a present, but if it is a book, do you think it could be NOT about God, because I know everything about Him!"

Princess Elizabeth was a great favorite of her grandfather, King George V—"Grandpapa England," as she called him. The two were once found on hands and knees peering under a sofa in an attempt to find a lost hairslide.

Once at a Sandringham Christmas party, the whole royal family were listening to carol singers. Mishearing the words "Tidings of great joy I bring to you and all mankind," Princess Elizabeth ran across the room to King George and said: "I know that 'old man kind.' That's YOU, Grandpapa England. You are old, and you are very, very kind."

Princess Margaret Rose, Her Majesty the Queen and the Princess Elizabeth are presented above in a strikingly attractive picture. The Queen is holding the hand of Princess Elizabeth and has her arm about Princess Margaret Rose, a pose typical of this happy family.

Is Proficient In Music and Some of Arts

The Queen Has Endeavored to Bring Up Daughters to Enjoy Family Life and Routine of Other Girls.

The death of the King was a great sorrow to his granddaughter, who looked pale and awestruck as she attended the funeral service at Windsor and curtsied her last good-bye.

The two Princesses follow an established routine in their daily life. Both get up at 7:30 a.m., and breakfast in the nursery. At 9 o'clock they visit their parents, but lessons begin sharp at 9:15. There is a break for refreshments—glasses of orange juice—at 11 o'clock, and Princess Margaret's lessons are over for the day, while her sister works on till 12:30.

Lunches With Parents.

Princess Elizabeth lunches with her parents at 1:15, and when the royal family is at Royal Lodge, Windsor, Princess Margaret joins them in the dining-room. In London she still has lunch and tea in the schoolroom. As much of the afternoon as possible is spent out of doors, and tea is at a quarter to five.

The hour from 5:30 to 6:30 is always spent in the Queen's sitting-room unless some public engagement obliges her to be out, in which case the children play games in the schoolroom.

Princess Margaret's bedtime is twenty minutes past six, and Princess Elizabeth follows her sister upstairs at a quarter past seven. About a quarter of an hour later, the King and Queen go up to the nursery together to say goodnight to their daughters.

Her Good Manners.

Much could be written about the charm and natural manners of the heir to the British throne. Once at one of her sister's birthday parties, a visitor committed the terrible crime of refusing a slice of the birthday cake. Apologizing humbly for this mistake, which had profoundly shocked Princess Elizabeth, he explained that he had not realized it was the BIRTHDAY cake.

Princess Elizabeth at once rose to the occasion. "It was my fault," she said; "I ought to have told you."

Her apparent freedom from shyness is due neither to insensitiveness nor to over-confidence, but to self-control.

"Were you shy?" she was asked after some rather formidable occasion.

"Oh, yes! I was," she answered, "I am afraid I am getting shy, but I MUSTN'T be shy. I wish I were more like Mummie!"

This candor and self-mastery in a girl of Princess Elizabeth's age surely contain the best of auguries for the future.

Loyal Messages of Greeting From Ottawa Valley C

COUNTY wardens, mayors and reeves of the Ottawa Valley have sent The Citizen loyal messages of greeting to Their Majesties on behalf of the citizens in their municipalities. They are given herewith:

Carleton County

CARLETON County, in unison with every Canadian municipality across the Dominion, extends its greetings to Their Gracious Majesties and expresses profound pleasure on the occasion of their visit. In behalf of all the people of this far-flung county, settled first by British stock, I bespeak our warm gratitude and our steadfast loyalty.

STUART CRAIG,
Warden.

Gatineau County

GATINEAU County is most happy to proffer to Their Majesties expressions of loyalty, gratitude and satisfaction on the occasion of their forthcoming visit to Canada. The hope of all our people is that they may reign long and happily and that every citizen of the British Empire stands ready in every crisis to defend all Their Majesties represent.

EDWARD McNALLY,
Warden.

Papineau County

AS warden of the historic county of Papineau I take pleasure and great honor in issuing in behalf of all our people a hearty welcome and sincere greetings to our noble King and gracious Queen for their generous visit to Canada. May God bless their journey and protect them throughout.

THEO. CORBEIL,
Warden.

Leeds and Grenville

ON this most auspicious occasion of the visit of Their Majesties, our beloved King and Queen, I embrace this opportunity of expressing on behalf of the people of the united counties of Leeds and Grenville our loyal and deep devotion and appreciation of our British heritage. God Save the King!

W. E. LATIMER,
Warden.

Lanark County

THE warden and members of the Council of the County of Lanark respectfully desire to express their loyalty to Their Majesties on the occasion of their visit to Canada, and their hope that the time spent here may be pleasant and enjoyable.

JAS. A. GUTHRIE,
Warden.

Renfrew County

I AM duly appreciative of the honor of extending to our beloved King and Queen a sincere welcome from all people in this county of Renfrew. Our prayer is that their sejourn with us will be happy, safe and impressive of the love Canadians everywhere bear toward their persons and toward the British throne.

ALBERT WALLACE,
Warden.

Prescott and Russell

THE United Counties of Russell and Prescott, upon whose shores Champlain tarried, where Seigneur de Longueuil once dwelt and Indians and fur traders bartered their wares, where much of the language and many of the customs are still those of old France, are profoundly impressed and deeply grateful for the visit of King George VI and Queen Elizabeth. Nowhere in all Canada's nine provinces will hearts beat faster or warmer in welcome anticipation than in these pioneer counties and I express the love, loyalty and welcome of all the people, without distinction of nationality, creed or class.

JOSEPH MORIN,
Warden.

Dundas, Stormont and Glengarry

THESE United Counties of Dundas, Stormont and Glengarry, whose pioneer settlers along the historic St. Lawrence river included many United Empire Loyalists, whose shore line is plentifully dotted with monuments and tablets recalling many outstanding military and national achievements, are more united than ever on this occasion as they proclaim in unison their affection of all people to their beloved King and Queen and humbly bid Their Majesties welcome.

ROBERT BRYAN,
Warden.

Pontiac County

FROM the hills and valleys of this great county of Pontiac in Quebec, from the density of its forest land and the cavernous depths of its mines there comes today from all people in this expansive territory spontaneous welcome to Their Majesties King George VI and Queen Elizabeth.

ROBERT B. CARSWELL,
Warden.

Prescott

ON behalf of the citizens of the Corporation of the Town of Prescott I wish to welcome Their Majesties on the occasion of their unprecedented visit to the New World.

It is a happy augury of continued loyal relations between this majestic Dominion and the British Isles, as well as an opportunity for closer understanding between our good neighboring republic and the Empire in the march towards universal peace and the brotherhood of man, and it is our sincere wish that Their Majesties, King George VI and Queen Elizabeth, will obtain this impression in our midst.

JOHN T. HORAN,
Mayor.

Arnprior

THE great honor that is bestowed on Canada by the visit of Your Most Gracious Majesties is appreciated by every Canadian in all parts of the Dominion. The citizens of Arnprior are proud to be a part of the great Empire on which the sun never sets and we are happy to pledge to Your Majesties our deepest loyalty and to express the hope that your visit will be most pleasant.

A. H. REID,"
Mayor.

North Bay

ON behalf of the citizens of North Bay, "Gateway of the North," we extend a most sincere welcome to Their Majesties on this, their first visit to our beloved country, and give assurance of our people's unswerving fidelity towards the truth and the freedom which Their Majesties so faithfully represent.

A. BEATTIE,
Mayor.

Almonte

THE citizens of Almonte consider it a great honor to join with the rest of this fair British Dominion in extending to Their Majesties, our King and Queen, a cordial welcome on the occasion of their visit. Long may they reign.

W. W. WATCHORN,
Mayor.

Smiths Falls

ON the occasion of the visit of Their Majesties King George VI and Queen Elizabeth, on behalf of the citizens of the town of Smiths Falls we send our greetings and a loyal welcome, and wish Their Majesties a vacation full of enjoyment.

J. J. BRADLEY,
Mayor.

Renfrew Town

THE citizens of Renfrew greet Their Majesties with heartfelt loyalty, recognizing in them the embodiment of the Empire's genius and solidarity and viewing their visit as an augury of a greater Canada and Empire, secure in freedom, strong in righteousness and happy in the rule of Their Majesties, George and Elizabeth.

ROBERT BURTON,
Acting Mayor.

Carleton Place

THE loyal citizens of the town of Carleton Place, proud of their British connection, delighting in the freedom and justice of British institutions, welcome with joy and gratitude Their Majesties King George VI and Queen Elizabeth to Canada and proffe[r] them their humble duty and affection.

W. ASA ROE,
Mayor.

Vankleek Hill

ON behalf of the citizens of the to[wn of] Vankleek Hill I have the ho[nor to] extend to Their Gracious Majesties [a] hearty welcome. Here, where the [two] dominant Canadian races dwell to[gether in] harmony, we join in assuring ou[r] King and Queen of our continu[ed loyalty] and devotion.

D. A. IR[...]

Perth

REALIZING the impossibil[...] of Perth to be honor[...] visit from Your Majestie[s ...] loyalty and affection, whic[h ...] on such an occasion, by [...] happiness and prosperit[y ...] reign, which, we pray, [...] long.

G. C. [...]

Ganc[...]

ON behalf of the [...] Gananoque, it [...] to extend to Thei[r ...] Queen, a sincere [...] on the occasion [...]

THE peop[...] many t[...] day as one [...] welcome [...] Queen. [...]

(Far left)

Ottawa Evening Citizen,
May 16, 1939.
Photo by Anthony Scullion,
courtesy National Library
of Canada.

(Left)

Queen Elizabeth with
Princess Anne on her seventh
birthday, 1957.
Photo by Lord Snowdon,
Camera Presse/PonoPresse.

(Right)

Untitled, 1955.
Work by Pietro Annigoni,
Camera Presse/PonoPresse.

I THINK MANY YOUNG PEOPLE TODAY ARE SEEKING A KIND OF SPIRITUALITY THAT

WILL HELP THEM DEAL WITH A WORLD THAT OFTEN SEEMS TO BE FALLING APART. WITH

THE SHATTERING EVENTS IN THE BALKANS, IN KOSOVO, IN WHAT HAPPENED IN AFRICA

TO THE TUTSIS, MANY PEOPLE ARE ANGUISHING AND AT A LOSS AS TO HOW TO MAKE

SENSE OF THE EVENTS OF THE WORLD.

IN THE THEATRE, THROUGH THE ART OF THE "PAROLE," I SEE MY STUDENTS FIND

MEANING AND CONNECTION, STRUGGLE TO TELL THEIR TRUTHS AND TO CONVEY THEM

TO THE AUDIENCE. IN THIS WAY, I THINK THEY DISCOVER THE SPIRITUALITY THEY

ARE SEEKING.

Monique Mercure, actor

Whitewater rafting on
Quebec's Rivière Rouge.
Photo by Francis Lépine,
Biosphère Photographie.

ARTS AND LEISURE

Canadians have transcended the borders of this country in all aspects of the arts: dance, song, painting, cinema, literature, journalism and even architecture. Whether our artistry is fuelled by ambition, talent, humour, or simply by the burning desire to create, there's no question that Canadians are at the forefront of artistic endeavour.

Just in 1999, we can cite the achievements of rock, pop, and country singers Alanis Morissette, Céline Dion and Shania Twain who together took home six Grammy Awards, the American Recording Academy's highly coveted prize for excellence in music.

We can cite the eight Genies given (also in 1999) to the *The Red Violin*, directed by François Girard, and the work of director Norman Jewison, who took top honours at the Oscars for such award-winning work as *Fiddler on the Roof, Moonstruck* and *In the Heat of the Night*.

Meanwhile, established novelists such as Michael Ondaatje, Mordecai Richler, Michel Tremblay and Carol Shields continue to receive accolades for their fiction at home and abroad.

Short story collections by Alice Munro and Diane Schoemperlen have now been awarded, respectively, the Giller Prize and the Governor General's Literary Award. Another generation of writers—from Anne Michaels and Jane Urquhart in Ontario to Vancouver Island's Gail Anderson-Dargatz and Quebec's Robert Lalonde—is also attracting the interest of readers and critics.

In dance, the Royal Winnipeg Ballet, inspired for years by the ethereal spirit of prima ballerina Evelyn Hart, continues to make headlines with its mixture of classical and contemporary dance. In 1998, the RWB staged *Dracula* with such panache that the company's subscriptions went up by 30% from the year before.

We can also cite the achievement of Canadian architects such as Ernest Cormier, who designed the Supreme Court of Canada (built in the 1940s) and whose work foretold the age of modernism in this field. Following in his footsteps, Arthur Erikson became the first Canadian architect to achieve international recognition with such feats as Simon Fraser University.

In broadcasting, the voices of Foster Hewitt, Jack Webster, Gaétan Girouard and Barbara Frum still echo in our collective memories, while viewers and listeners across the country continue to tune in to Peter Gzowski, Pamela Wallin, Peter Mansbridge, Robert-Guy Scully, Pierre Bruneau and Lloyd Robertson, to name only a few.

Despite its sparse population, Canada's North is also well-peopled with artists from many fields. The pencil drawings of birds, fish and headless giants of Cape Dorset artist Sheojuk Etidlooie, for example, are treasured in collections around the world. Artisans in the small community of Baker Lake, along the northwestern shores of Hudson Bay, produce exquisite stone carvings and wall hangings.

Canada's artistic achievements are rooted in our history. In the late 19th century, Quebec's Emma Albani became one of Europe's premier opera stars—the first Canadian to achieve such international fame. Toronto's Mary Pickford, known as "America's Sweetheart," was *the* star of the silent film era. During the 1960s, coffee houses such as Calgary's

Depression, Winnipeg's 4D, the Village Corner in Toronto and Montréal's Café Finjan introduced audiences to new performers such as Joni Mitchell, Neil Young, Ian and Sylvia, and Kate and Anna McGarrigle.

In addition to achievement in the arts, Canada's history books are rich with the accomplishments of amateur and professional athletes. In our Olympian arenas, we have produced stars of heroic dimension including Silken Laumann, who sculled to an Olympic bronze medal in the face of great physical pain and, at the 1996 Olympics, Donovan Bailey, who set a new world record as "the fastest man in the world."

There is no doubt many of our national heroes have been our hockey players and the world of hockey is richer for Howie Morenz, Maurice "Rocket" Richard, Jean Beliveau, Bobby Orr, Guy Lafleur, Gordie Howe, Ken Dryden, Mario Lemieux and Wayne Gretzky.

Yet, despite these many accomplishments, there is also something in the Canadian psyche that makes us ambivalent about the success of our artists. "Ironically enough," Oscar Peterson noted, "I had to leave Canada and immerse myself in the American field of jazz in order to gain my credentials, so to speak, in that medium."

This contradiction may be best summed up by author Margaret Atwood: "If your book does very well, you will receive three nasty vicious personal attacks from people you've never met, in print, within the year," she writes. "Don't take them personally. They aren't personal. They are just part of the time-honoured tradition of cutting the legs off people who grow fast—especially beloved by Canadians, but observed elsewhere as well."

The Performing Arts

In the early 1980s, one of Canada's leading choreographers, Robert Desrosiers, was asked to create a dance for the National Ballet of Canada. *The Blue Snake* featured a futuristic ballet of zebra-like dancers who flee the hands of giant puppets. This evocative ballet remains a signature piece of Canadian innovation in dance.

Innovative though we may be, dance companies in Canada generally operate at a financial loss. There are currently 91 surveyed dance companies, all non-profit, and due partly to a drop in both government subsidies and private donations, they are largely in the red. Nonetheless, from modern dance to classical ballet, dance companies enjoyed a surge of popular support in the late 1990s. In 1996–97, more than 1.3 million tickets were sold to more than 3,000 dance performances, an increase of 6% from two years before.

In Canada, there are no fewer than 24 opera companies, ranging from the Pacific Opera Victoria to L'Opéra du Québec to Opera New Brunswick and despite carrying the highest operating deficit of all performing arts companies, our orchestras continue to dazzle audiences. In 1996–97, the 145 orchestral groups surveyed gave some 3.4 million performances.

In terms of sheer numbers, Quebec has the most active dramatic community in the country with companies ranging from Le Théâtre du Nouveau Monde to Théâtre Ubu. In 1996–97, for example, the province had 155 theatre companies, far more than any other province.

LES CANADIENS

Written by Rick Salutin with an assist by Ken Dryden
Directed by George Luscombe   Designed by Astrid Janson
Oct 20 thru Nov 19 every eve 8.30 pm Sunday Matinees 2.30 pm
TWP Theatre 12 Alexander Street Telephone 925-8640
A Toronto Workshop Production

In 1958, John Hirsch and Tom Hendry created the Manitoba Theatre Centre, considered the first regional theatre in the country. Through the years, its vibrant repertoire has toured across Canada, and in 1995, a production of *Hamlet*, starring Canadian-bred Keanu Reeves, made international headlines.

Today, the Manitoba Theatre Centre is joined by theatres such as Vancouver Sath, which stages work about the lives of the Punjabi community, Buddies in Bad Times Theatre in Toronto, which explores issues relevant to gays and lesbians, and the Neptune Theatre in Halifax, which stages local plays and musicals, often with a Maritime theme.

Books

Canadian authors and writers have established Canada as an international literary force. One indication of this vigour is to be found in the publishing industry.

Today, there are some 562 book publishers and exclusive agents in Canada. Of these, 529 are Canadian-owned and account for almost two-thirds of the $2 billion in revenue generated by the industry in 1996–97. On the other hand, Canadian publishers and agents aren't nearly as profitable as the foreign-controlled companies that operate on Canadian soil.

With agents demanding high advances and U.S. publishing rights, profit margins for Canadian companies are small. On the other hand, while few Canadians may realize it, Harlequin Enterprises—creators of the "Harlequin Romance" novel—is a Canadian publisher. In 1998, it sold more than 165 million books worldwide.

Magazines and Newspapers

Canada has 104 daily newspapers—60 of them owned by the Southam-Hollinger group. Southam-Hollinger's papers reach 2.4 million Canadian households every day—accounting for nearly 43% of total newspaper circulation. In addition to our newspapers, we are avid readers of magazines.

From the early days of publishing, Canadian magazines have competed with titles from the United States. For example, when Canada's *The Literary Garland* folded in the early 1800s, one of its contributing writers, Susanna Moodie, lamented that it was "utterly impossible" to combat American monthlies which were "handsomely illustrated, composed of the best articles . . . and sold at such a low rate."

Today, foreign magazines, mostly from the United States, represent 80% of the titles on our newsstands, and half of all sales. Since the mid-1960s, Canada has protected the magazine industry from so-called split-run editions—periodicals that are prepared in the United States, but published as a "Canadian" edition. Canadian publishers believe that our magazines are at risk because split-run editions can offer Canadian advertisers better rates than similar Canadian periodicals.

However, in 1997, the World Trade Organization ruled that measures we use to protect the industry, such as excise taxes and tariffs on foreign publications, contravene international agreements. Two years later, Canada complied with the ruling, and as

"If we are to read good books with a full understanding, and still more, if we attempt to produce literature ourselves, we must preserve a clean and fastidious palate. Our sense of values must be at once austere and catholic. We should be able to appreciate good writing of every kind."

Lord Tweedsmuir, 1940

(Right)
Author Margaret Laurence,
at home, Lakefield, Ontario,
1975.
Photo by John Reeves.

the *Portrait* went to press, Canadian and American officials were grappling over the amount of Canadian content that would be required of American publications aimed at the Canadian market.

In 1996–97, there were 1,552 Canadian-published periodicals—about 200 fewer titles than in the early 1990s. However, these magazines were earning higher revenues and profits. In fact, in 1996–97, total revenues surpassed $1 billion.

French-language magazines, which are actually more profitable than English-language magazines, rely less on advertising and more on newsstand sales for revenue. In 1996–97, for example, advertising accounted for 66% of revenue for English-language magazines, but never averaged more than 50% of revenues for French titles.

While Canadian magazines come and go, several of those established in the early decades of the 20th century have survived to become vehicles for our best writers and mainstays of our culture. *Saturday Night*, *Maclean's* and *L'actualité* have played important roles in the political and cultural life of Canada. In the 1940s, for example, three decades before his Deptford trilogy established him as a major novelist, Robertson Davies wrote for *Saturday Night*. In the 1950s and 1960s, *Maclean's* featured the journalism of Pierre Berton, Hugh Garner, Peter Newman and Peter Gzowski, and novelist Mordecai Richler also wrote for *Maclean's* and remains a contributing editor to *Saturday Night*.

Film

Just as American magazines fill up our

newsstands, foreign films have traditionally taken up most of the screen time in our movie theatres. Foreign-owned subsidiaries, which dominate the film distribution industry, have shown little interest in distributing or marketing Canadian films, and our films have a difficult time finding venues in our own country. (One noteworthy exception was *The Red Violin*.)

Despite many challenges, Canadian movies do get made and continue to make a splash around the world. At the 1997 film festival in Cannes, for example, a sell-out crowd watched *Kissed*, the debut feature from Lynne Stopkewich. That same year, filmmaker Atom Egoyan won three awards at the prestigious festival for *The Sweet Hereafter*, including the Grand Prix. All the international acclaim helps sell our films abroad. In 1996–97, we exported some $362 million of independent films, videos and audio-visuals, more than double the amount sold in 1992–93.

In addition to these contemporary successes, we can also look back over the last three decades to find similarly important cinematic milestones. In the early 1960s, *À Tout Prendre*, the first feature film by Quebec director, writer and actor Claude Jutra, won several international awards, setting the stage for later Jutra films such as the classic *Mon Oncle Antoine*.

We also export our talent, and a long line of Canadians have found success in Hollywood: directors Norman Jewison, David Cronenberg and James Cameron and actors Michael J. Fox, Leslie Nielsen and Jim Carrey.

Partly owing to a favourable exchange rate and tax credits, Canada attracts film producers from all over the world. In 1997, for example, some 167 productions—domestic and foreign—were shot in Vancouver, including 24 feature films and 53 movies-of-the-week. Between the late 1970s and 1997, the value of film and television production in British Columbia grew from $17.5 million to $630 million.

Television

Canada is the world's second-largest exporter of television programs. (First comes the United States.) Our shows are popular the world over; "Due South," for example, was the highest rated foreign program on Britain's BBC in 1998.

Production activity is mostly based in Toronto, Montréal and Vancouver with results like "Traders," "Ces enfants d'ailleurs" and "Cold Squad." Canadian industry also often hosts foreign producers, particularly from the United States. American programs such as "The X-Files" and "Kung Fu: The Legend Continues," for example, have been shot in Canada.

We've been watching slightly less television over the past decade, with the exception of 1995, when new specialty and pay-TV cable channels were introduced. In 1997, we spent an average of 22.7 hours a week in front of the television, which included about 1.3 hours watching videotapes. This is a slight decrease from 1988 when we watched an average of 23.5 hours of TV a week.

The francophones of Quebec are the most avid viewers of television; they watch an average of 26 hours each week. In 1996, francophones—who do not have the same range of foreign programming in their language as anglophones—spent two-thirds of their television-viewing time watching Canadian shows. Anglophones, on the other hand, spent less than a third of their TV time watching homemade fare.

Television's top draw in Quebec continues to be "La petite vie," a spoof of the typical Quebec family. Episodes of "La petite vie" regularly draw viewers in the 4-million range. In the 1950s, a television program called "La famille Plouffe" had a similar following, its premise being the trials and tribulations of a traditional Quebec working-class family.

Radio and Recordings

On a December evening in 1938, at the Emmanuel Presbyterian Church in Toronto, a six-year-old boy with perfect pitch delighted the audience with his second public performance on the piano. Shortly after this performance, Glenn Gould began telling people that he would become a concert pianist.

Whether it's Gould's interpretations of Johann Sebastian Bach, the pop songs of Sarah McLachlan or the "living fiddle" of Ashley MacIsaac, Canada has a long history of producing distinctive recording artists. Yet for all the success of our musicians, the Canadian sound recording industry is dominated by multinational firms, also known as "the majors."

Fiddler Lisa MacIsaac, Creigniche, Nova Scotia. Self-portrait by David Trattles.

In 1995–96, for example, there were 15 such majors, and collectively they produced nearly 4,700 recordings—more than double the number released by 239 Canadian-owned companies. Still, Canadian companies tend to nurture home-grown talent: in 1995–96, some 80% of the more than 800 new recordings featuring Canadian-born artists were released by Canadian-owned firms.

There are dramatic differences between our English- and French-language recording industries. In Quebec, the vast majority of French-language compact discs, audiocassettes and the like are distributed by independent, Quebec-based companies. In the rest of Canada, just the opposite is true: the majors distribute most of the English-language recordings.

In the late 1990s, Canada's copyright laws were being revised to ensure that songwriters, composers and music publishers were adequately compensated for the electronic reproduction of their works. Some cultural observers have suggested that the careers of artists such as Anne Murray and The Guess Who were "vaulted into another dimension" by "CanCon" legislation. According to this 1971 law, AM radio stations are required to play at least 30% Canadian content, or CanCon, between the hours of 6 a.m. and midnight.

The Airwaves

Canadian radio is a mix of private and public stations. The publicly funded Canadian Broadcasting Corporation (CBC) broadcasts on two networks: Radio One and Radio Two, and there are campus and community radio stations spread across the country. In 1997, for example, the Vancouver Public Aquarium Association received a licence to broadcast the whistles, yelps and squeaks of killer whales on ORCA FM.

Some 575 private radio stations broadcast a variety of formats—from "oldies" to country music to easy listening. In 1997, country music was the format of choice for more than half of Newfoundland's listeners while nearly half of radio listeners in Ontario preferred adult contemporary and "oldies."

Overall, Canadians listen to radio less and less, but how much we listen depends on various factors. In 1997, for example, women in Prince Edward Island who were 60 years of age and older were the most avid listeners, spending nearly nine hours more a week than our national average of about 20 hours. However, anglophone men in Quebec between 25 and 34 years old were not far behind: they spent an average of 26 hours a week listening to radio.

Comedian Mary Walsh "interviews" skater Elvis Stojko at Skate Canada in Halifax, Nova Scotia, 1997. Photo by Andrew Vaughan, Canapress Photo Service.

STAR STRUCK In 1896, the first kiss ever recorded in a moving picture was screened in an Ottawa park for an audience of some 1,200. The star behind the pucker was the 33-year-old Canadian May Irwin, and the star struck was the American actor John Rice. The film lasted less than one minute. Although its contents were denounced (it was considered racy for the mores of the day), it nonetheless marked the beginning of Canada's long love affair with the movies. Like many love affairs, this romance has variously burned brightly, then dimly. It reached its height in 1952–53, when Canadians purchased 256 million tickets to the movies; that's as if everyone in the country had been to the movies 18 times over. With the appearance of television, however, interest in the movies cooled. By the early 1960s, admissions had fallen by 62%; in 1963–64, Canadians purchased fewer than 98 million tickets to the flicks.

The 1990s have been a curious movie era. In 1991–92, Canadians bought only about 72 million tickets, but by the late 1990s, our affair seemed to blossom again. In 1996–97, some 92 million tickets were purchased, the same as if everyone went off to the movies three times over. This pattern almost exactly mirrors the American movie-going experience. In 1991, movie attendance in the United States dipped to 1.1 billion, but in 1997, it reached 1.4 billion, the same as if every American had gone off to the movies five times.

These cinematic trends are partly due to the decline of the cocooning era, when all North Americans settled into their living rooms with remote controls, VCRs and various other home entertainment gadgets. Now, as the baby boomers' children are growing up, parents are once again free to catch a flick, and their kids—in their teens and twenties—are also eager moviegoers. In addition, the face of the movie industry has altered enormously. There's a significant trend towards multiple-screen theatres that offer bigger, curved screens, stadium seating and digital sound, not to mention video games in the lobbies and a wide selection of snacks, including fast food.

Somewhere between the first cinematic kiss in a park in Ottawa and these new movie halls, Canada has lost a generation of single-screen theatres. These were the old-style Hollywood palaces with their one big screen, draped curtains, velvet-covered chairs and frescos and oil paintings across wide domed interiors. The air redolent with the aroma of popcorn, these movie houses also held us in their thrall and their passing marks the end of another kind of movie romance.

May Irwin and John Rice in *The Widow Jones*, 1896.
Photo courtesy U.S. Department of the Interior, National Park Service, Edison National Historic Site.

Woodbine Race Track,

Toronto, Ontario, 1956.

Photo by Lutz Dille, courtesy

Canadian Museum of

Contemporary Photography.

POTATO CINEMA Canadians watch an average of three hours and 12 minutes of television every day. In almost every Canadian household, there is at least one colour television, and in every second home, two or more. Cable adds the dimension of plenty: in 1997, about 8 million Canadian households subscribed to cable television.

All of this home entertainment led Faith Popcorn, the American trend-spotter, to coin the phrase "cocooning." Another popular phrase "the couch potato" describes our inclination to home entertainment. In Canada, one in five households now reports owning more than one VCR and as recently as 1997, Canadians used VCRs to watch the equivalent of one feature film per week.

Another frequently used home entertainment gadget is the CD player. In 1988, a mere 8% of households owned one. By 1997, more than half of Canada's households owned a CD player.

In 1992, only 20% of Canadian households owned a home computer. By 1997, this had increased to 36%. In a single year, between 1996 and 1997, the number of Canadian households reporting Internet use at home nearly doubled from 7% to 13%. Some industry experts have ranked Canada fifth in the world—behind the United States, Japan, the United Kingdom and Germany—in terms of sheer numbers of Internet users. In 1998, nearly 6.5 million Canadians regularly surfed the Internet at home or at work.

THE PENCIL has been described as "the first chronicler of new-born thought." The first known reference to the pencil dates to 1565 when a German physician named Konrad Gesner found occasion to write: "The stylus shown here is made for writing . . . from a sort of lead . . . shaved to a point and inserted in a wooden handle."

The pencil is quite possibly our most ubiquitous writing instrument. A tool of the artist, the architect, schoolchildren and jotters everywhere, the pencil's chief charm may be its forgiving nature; its jottings can always be erased.

In 1994, the most recent year for which statistics are available, Canada's four pencil-manufacturing plants produced more than three pencils for every Canadian. In all, they manufactured 97,718,400 pencils and pencil crayons, valued at $12.8 million. Compared with its fellow writer, the ballpoint pen, the Canadian pencil leads the way in volume and market value. In 1994, Canada's six ballpoint-pen manufacturers produced almost one pen for every Canadian— some 26,113,764 pens in all. Their total value was only slightly less than that of pencils at $12.4 million.

The humble pencil is one word processor and graphic design tool that will always be Y2K compliant, and needs no user's manual, no technical help line, no peripherals, no mouse, no cables, no surge protector—just a simple sharpener or knife. If there is one humble, hand-held innovation that will surely endure, it must be the pencil.

Former Mining Town
Becomes a Learning Centre
for Industrial Archaeologists,
1986.
Work by Eleanor Bond, in
charcoal, from *Work Station.*

Visual Arts

On November 17, 1927, Vancouver artist Emily Carr travelled to Toronto to meet, for the first time, Harris, MacDonald, Varley, Jackson, Lismer, Johnston and Carmichael—collectively known as the Group of Seven. "Oh these men, this Group of Seven, what have they created?" she wrote in her journal. "A world stripped of earthiness, shorn of fretting details, purged, purified; a naked soul, pure and unashamed; lovely space filled with wonderful serenity. What language do they speak, those silent, awe-filled spaces?"

Canada's Group of Seven created a fair scandal in their day. Critics and art lovers alike were confounded by their new art.

Today, the language of Canadian art continues to intrigue and engage its audiences and is on view in a broad assortment of public and private galleries across the country—from the Art Gallery of Nova Scotia in Halifax to the National Gallery of Canada in Ottawa to the Surrey Art Gallery in British Columbia. In addition, Canada has a network of artist-run centres, including one in Calgary simply called Truck.

Of all the "cultural workers," visual artists have the lowest annual income. They earn on average $14,000 a year, and almost half of this income comes from other jobs. In 1997, more than 136,000 Canadians worked in the visual arts and artistic design field, a jump of 33% from a decade before.

Canada's Heritage

In the words of the first commissioner of the National Parks of Canada (J.B. Harkin), recorded sometime between 1911 and 1936, our parks "exist that every citizen of Canada may satisfy his craving for nature and nature's beauty; that he may absorb the poise and restfulness of the forests; that he may steep his soul in the brilliance of the wild flowers and the sublimity of the mountain peaks."

This vision of Canada's wild spaces continues today. With 38 national parks, the forests and lakes of Canada remain safe havens for wildlife, Canadians and all peoples of the world who care to visit. Someone on a "bison creep" at the Wood Buffalo National Park in the Northwest Territories, for example, can see the world's largest herd of free-roaming bison. In the Georgian Bay Islands National Park in Ontario, kayakers slip into secluded bays and inlets and backpackers in Pacific Rim National Park on Vancouver Island trek through dense rainforests.

In 1995–96, Canadians and foreigners made some 58 million visits to our interpretive nature parks and conservation areas. Between 1989 and 1995, the number of visitors to the four mountain parks of Banff, Jasper, Kootenay and Yoho jumped by 26%.

Alongside our system of parks, we have museums, archives, libraries and historic sites, as well as planetariums, aquariums and zoos. In 1995–96, these institutions attracted more than 54 million visitors both from Canada and abroad, a slight decrease from the early 1990s.

(Above)
Beach boardwalk,
Bouctouche, New Brunswick.
Photo by Gilles Daigle, Multi
Images Inc.

(Right)
Artist Jack Shadbolt, 1996.
Photo by Rob Kruyt.

"A performance is not a contest

but a love affair."

Glenn Gould

While public funding may not be keeping up with operating costs, overall revenue from admissions increased 68% between 1989–90 and 1995–96, to $91 million. In museums, for example, revenue from gift shops and concessions almost doubled.

The Sport of Leisure

Some 92% of Canadians aged 12 years and older get exercise in some form. The most common activity for both men and women is walking, but swimming, bicycling and workouts at home are also popular. When it comes to physical activity, men prefer hockey and golf while women would rather take an aerobics class.

While some sports flit in and out of fashion, our passion for hockey stands the test of time. Even before the turn of the 20th century, hockey had become Canada's most popular winter team sport. The tradition of watching "Hockey Night in Canada" on CBC Television on Saturday evenings has become so entrenched that the opening theme has been called our unofficial national anthem. Today, some 2 million Canadians play hockey in more than 3,000 arenas. It's Canada's most popular sport, played regularly by about 6% of adults.

For all its cultural and economic significance, sport is just one of the many ways we spend our leisure time. In fact, people are going out less often to arenas and stadiums. In 1996, some 22% of households bought tickets to live sporting events, a drop of 5% over the previous decade.

We are travelling more, especially to heritage sites such as national parks. In 1997, we took 13.5 million leisure trips of one or more nights that involved visiting a heritage site. We also like to garden, spending $1.1 billion on floriculture and nursery products in 1997—the highest amount ever.

We like to read. An international study noted that more than 70% of university-educated Canadians spent time reading a book each week.

Increasingly, we also like to gamble. In 1997, we wagered $6.8 billion on some form of government-run gambling activity, more than twice as much money as we gambled in 1992. Part of the increase is due to the growth of casinos, lotteries and video lottery terminals in most provinces.

Demographic experts have predicted that when baby boomers—those born between 1946 and 1966—reach their fifties in the early 21st century, they will have a major impact on leisure activities such as travel and sport. If patterns hold over the next few decades, travellers aged 51 to 60 will account for almost one-third of travel spending.

Since "mature travellers" now make up one-quarter of the visitors to heritage sites, there may be still greater interest in our museums and galleries. At the same time, an aging population may be less likely to latch on downhill skis and more likely to tee up on the golf course. Demographic experts predict that less strenuous activities such as birding, walking and gardening will increase in popularity in the early decades of the 21st century.

(Left)
Skater Barbara Ann Scott,
Ottawa, Ontario, 1946.
Photo by Yousuf Karsh,
courtesy National Archives
of Canada, PA-160309

SIR John A. Macdonald had the right idea with his National Policy.

Virtually every major industrial power in the world today began its life behind high tariff walls. From the 1880s to 1947, tariffs allowed Canada to get on her feet, so to speak, and for our industrial roots to strengthen and grow.

But as our economy has matured, we have slowly taken these walls down, first through the GATT, which began in 1947, then with the FTA in 1988 and now, with the NAFTA. Today, Canada is a leading industrial power.

We're on our own two feet in tough global competition. Our exports account for more of our wealth and jobs than ever before. To a great extent, and even to an ironic extent, this is Macdonald's legacy to us.

Richard Lipsey, economics professor

(Opposite page) Work by Wanda Koop. Photo by William Eakin.

Vancouver, British Columbia.

Photo by Stuart McCall,

Tony Stone.

THE ECONOMY

In 1911, the combined population of Toronto, Montréal and Vancouver was less than a million people. More than a third of the country's 2.72 million workers were earning their livelihood directly from the land. The average salary for factory workers was less than $500 per year and a pair of men's dress shoes could cost under $4.00. Wheat exports fuelled the economy and almost half of what was sold abroad went to Great Britain.

Canada's transition from this agricultural nation to a major economic power has been a remarkable one and bears the telling.

The story really begins shortly after Confederation, when Sir John A. Macdonald and his Conservative Party fought the election of 1878 with an economic blueprint for Canada they called the National Policy. Under their plan, free land would attract immigrant settlers to Prairie farms; the federal government would help construct a railway to tie the country together, and tariffs would protect Canadian goods from foreign competition. "Canada for the Canadians," Macdonald insisted, and his party won a resounding victory.

Although Sir John A. Macdonald did not live to see his vision of a National Policy become a reality, by the 1910s and 1920s, the die was cast in favour of his economic blueprint. Land-hungry immigrants had now begun to arrive in numbers not equaled before or since. Boarding trains in Halifax, Québec and Montréal, they headed for the "Last Best West," as the Prairies were then known. Once there, they provided a captive market for eastern factories and the Canadian Pacific Railway became a profitable venture, carrying goods to the West and wheat to the saltwater ports.

On New Year's Day 1914, one out of every 20 people in Canada had arrived the year before.

In these early days of Macdonald's National Policy, it took strong backs to keep our farms, mines, mills and factories running. Today, Canada has a well-educated labour force and one of the highest rates of postsecondary enrolment in the industrial world.

In 1996, some 40% of Canadian adults had completed college or university, compared with 29% in 1981. Today, the majority of jobs are in the service sector in keeping with the emergence of a global knowledge-based economy.

In 1998, Canada's gross domestic product or GDP (the value of all we produce) was $888 billion (at market prices) and Canadian families, on average, earned about $58,000. Incomes have just barely kept up with inflation and employment continues to be a problem. Since 1982, there have never been fewer than a million Canadians out of work, compared with an overall labour force of at least 12 million.

On the other hand, through the 1990s, price inflation virtually disappeared in Canada, and in 1998, consumer prices rose only 1%, even though the low Canadian dollar made imported goods more expensive.

Were Sir John A. to make an appearance in the Canada of the 1990s, he would find that fewer than 3% of the 15.6 million people in Canada's labour force work in agriculture and nearly 75% work in the service sector. He would find his Canada completely transformed. In 1996, truck driving was the most common occupation for men, while for women, it was retail sales.

Canada is now a huge exporter of goods and services, and manufactured goods—not wheat—lead the way. In 1998, exports of industrial goods, automobile products, machines and equipment, and consumer goods were worth almost $230 billion—more than nine times the value of farm exports. Our biggest export market by far for these goods is no longer Great Britain, as it was in the early part of the century, but the United States.

Booming exports have generated the foreign currency that we need to pay for imports. In 1998, Canadians bought $356 billion in goods and services from abroad, of which machines and equipment and automobile products were the largest components.

Today, we have the seventh largest economy among the industrialized nations. More impressive still, for five consecutive years in the 1990s, the United Nations has ranked Canada as the best country on the planet in which to live based on such factors as income, access to education and life expectancy.

Ownership and Control

The National Policy had truly begun to prove its worth by the time Canadians went to the polls in 1911. Nonetheless, the Liberal Party, which had been in power since 1896, called for a new economic direction, including free trade with the Americans. The Conservatives kept faith with Macdonald's vision and, on the campaign slogan "No truck nor trade with the Yankees," they were returned to power.

By the 1950s, the National Policy had made good on its promise of prosperity: Canada was well on the way to becoming one of the richest nations of the world. But the early dream of economic independence from the United States had not been fulfilled. In fact, just the opposite occurred.

As early as the 1920s, America began to overtake Britain as our largest export market. Since then, Canada and the United States have built the largest two-way trading relationship in the world. In 1998, some 84% of our exports were sold in the U.S. market, while 77% of our imports were "made in America." What's more, because of high Canadian tariffs on manufactured imports, it has often been more profitable for foreign companies to buy or build factories in Canada than to serve our market from their home countries. As a result, Americans have become huge investors in the Canadian economy. As early as 1926, some 30% of Canadian manufacturing was owned by American business.

Canadian Pacific poster,
c. 1930.
Courtesy Canadian Pacific
Archives, A-6022.

Through the 1950s and 1960s, U.S. capital fuelled Canada's economy. Companies expanded to meet growing demand for goods and services, creating millions of new jobs. By the 1960s, however, with 60% of our manufacturing and 70% of our oil and gas industries controlled from abroad, Canadians began to debate the benefits of foreign investment.

Economic nationalists talked of the silent surrender of Canada's economic sovereignty and Walter Gordon, Minister of Finance in the early 1960s, stated that "Canada is like a farmer who maintains his high standard of living by selling off another piece of the farm every spring." In 1974, the government created the Foreign Investment Review Agency to ensure that foreign takeovers and new investments offered a "significant benefit" to Canada.

Free Trade

If the debate over foreign ownership was a contentious issue in the 1960s and 1970s, it was mild compared with the free trade debate that began in the mid-1980s when Ottawa initiated negotiations with the United States. In one camp, labour unions and cultural and nationalist groups predicted dire consequences: lost jobs, falling wages, gutted social programs and the end of Canada's economic independence. "What is on the table is Canada itself," said Edmonton publisher Mel Hurtig. "What we're talking about is association-sovereignty," he declared. "We get the association, and the U.S. gets the sovereignty."

Most business leaders took an opposing view. They believed that open borders to the world's richest market would invigorate Canadian industry, attract investment and encourage growth. Among those who favoured free trade was the noted Canadian-born economist J.K. Galbraith who wrote: "Canadian sovereignty is not so slight a thing that it is really affected by greater purchases of gadgetry from the United States, with more lumber, newsprint and metal going south."

More than 10 years later, it is still difficult to separate the impact of free trade on the Canadian economy from other factors, such as globalization, changes in interest rates and government tax and spending policies. It is clear, however, that Canada and the United States have become partners in a single North American economy and, with the 1994 implementation of the North American Free Trade Agreement (NAFTA), Mexico became a third partner.

The east–west economic axis envisioned in the National Policy has shifted to the north and south, not just in terms of trade, but investment as well. As if to symbolize this shift, in 1997, Canadian National Railway spent $3.6 billion to gain control of the Illinois Central Railway, with its routes to the Gulf of Mexico. Between 1988 and 1998, Canadian firms increased their investments in American facilities by two-and-a-half times, to more than $126 billion.

Origins of Prosperity

Very early in this century, Canadians began moving to the cities to work in factories or in the service industries where they could earn more than they had on the farm. In 1900, about 37% of Canadians lived in cities and towns. By 1920, nearly 50% lived in urban areas and as the decade progressed, Canada found itself on a fairly solid economic footing. As world prices for raw materials firmed up, the farming, mining and forest industries prospered. Orders for machinery and equipment from the hinterland helped to sustain urban manufacturing, and the growing incomes of industrial workers encouraged rapid growth in the service sector. This was the National Policy in action.

Employment grew and living standards increased for most Canadians through the 1920s. Then suddenly, the roaring twenties ground to a halt. With the great stock market crash of 1929, came the first harbinger of impending crisis.

On October 29, or "Black Tuesday," the value of shares listed on the New York Stock Exchange fell by $14 billion, a tremendous sum at that time. In Canada, the Finance Department said that "the public ought to be reassured" and the next day, Prime Minister Mackenzie King boasted that "economic conditions have never been sounder, nor faith in the future greater."

Depression and War

Despite short-lived official optimism, tens of thousands of investors lost their life savings as the Montréal and Toronto Stock Exchanges followed Wall Street's lead. By 1932, the price of wheat was down to 54 cents a bushel. (In the mid-1920s, it had been $1.46.) Over the same period, prices for Canadian exports dropped by 42%. To make matters worse, an unprecedented drought in the early 1930s turned much of the prairie wheat lands into a dust bowl. Under attack by nature and world markets, many Canadian farmers were wiped out. Our mining, forestry and other primary industries also felt the twin blow of falling prices and rising U.S. tariffs, as the Americans tried to shield their own producers from a growing, worldwide economic collapse. As primary industries faltered, the manufacturing and service sectors were soon pulled into the downward spiral.

American President Harry Truman once described a recession as a time when "your neighbour loses his job." But a depression, he said, "is when you lose your own job." By 1933, more than 800,000 Canadians were out of work—an unemployment rate of 19%. For those who had jobs, wages and salaries fell by 25% between 1929 and 1933. The Great Depression, or the dirty thirties, was the bleakest period of our economic history. By 1933, the economy had shrunk by an incredible 30% and production did not return to pre-Depression levels until 1939. By then, Canada had begun to mobilize for war.

Explosive growth in the production of ships, tanks, aircraft, food and other vital war materials transformed Canada into an industrial power. Even though hundreds of thousands of men left their jobs to join in the fighting, Canadian factories ran at full capacity and manufacturing output more than doubled during the war years as women moved onto

"It was so dry in Saskatchewan during the Depression that the trees were chasing the dogs."

John G. Diefenbaker

(Top)

Cobalt, 1931.

Work by Yvonne McKague

Housser, courtesy National

Gallery of Canada.

(Bottom)

Toronto, Ontario, 1935.

Courtesy City of Toronto

Archives, James Collection,

2181.

Canadian Steel Foundries,
Montréal, Quebec, 1969,
from the series *Les ouvriers*
(The workers).
Photo by Pierre Gaudard,
courtesy Canadian Museum
of Contemporary
Photography.

shop floors in record numbers. Between 1938 and 1945, the female work force grew by 76% compared with just 4% growth in the male work force.

A Golden Age

Canada emerged from the war effort with its industrial base hugely expanded, while Japan and many European nations struggled to rebuild war-shattered economies. As peace returned, not only was the world hungry for our agricultural and resource products, but Canadian consumers now longed for goods that had not been available through the war years, or affordable during the Depression. According to a 1947 advertisement in *The Ottawa Citizen*, there was no doubt "a Ford in your future," and you could buy the "super deluxe" model for just over $1,500. Businesses thrived in this environment and for Canada's 12 million citizens, it was the dawn of the golden years.

Except for a slowdown in the late 1950s, Canada's economy grew steadily until the early 1970s. During the 1960s alone, GDP more than doubled while the unemployment rate averaged just 5% of the work force. Between 1945 and 1970, trade union membership tripled, helping to ensure that workers shared in the benefits of Canada's economic growth. From 1946 to 1975, average weekly wages grew from $32 to more than $200 although with rising consumer prices, pay cheques only went twice as far.

Canada's population also grew quickly. Throughout the 1950s, more than 1.5 million immigrants arrived, now headed for urban factories, offices and construction sites. But even more significant was Canada's baby boom, which continued into the 1960s. As the boomers boosted demand for houses, schools, cars, clothes and consumer products, the economy expanded. During the golden years, there was no shortage of investment money in Canada. Some came from domestic sources, while American investments in our industries increased more than tenfold.

As profits, wages and living standards rose steadily, money flowed into government coffers to pay for new programs. Between 1945 and 1969, total annual government expenditures on health care increased by 50 times, on education, by 30 times and on social welfare, by a factor of 13. The social safety net of medicare, old age security, subsidized university and college education and other programs was fashioned by Canadians who had survived the hardship of the Depression and war, and was financed by the prosperity and productivity of the golden years.

End of an Era

There are a number of theories on what brought these golden years to an end. Some blame the Organization of Petroleum Exporting Countries (OPEC), which tripled oil prices in 1973, sending a shock through the industrialized world. More than likely, it was a combination of factors that touched off

Moose Jaw, Saskatchewan.
Photo by Kevin Dunn,
courtesy Canapress Photo
Service.

an inflationary spiral in Canada in the early 1970s. Consumer prices, which had risen by less than 3% in 1971, were increasing at about 11% per year by 1974. Workers and unions fought for hefty pay increases to protect their living standards, but this just drove prices higher. Unemployment began to rise and more than 700,000 people, or 7.1% of the labour force, were out of work by 1975, the highest rate in 15 years.

The government attempted to regulate price and wage movement through a new agency, the Anti-Inflation Board (AIB). The AIB hired hundreds of workers to enforce its regulations, but its impact on inflation and unemployment was modest.

To add to the predicament, while the growth in tax revenue slowed down, government spending on unemployment insurance, welfare and other programs grew faster. To fill the gap, the federal and provincial governments began borrowing, and through the 1980s and early 1990s, public debt rose to levels not seen since the Second World War. The opposition parties charged that government spending was out of control.

In 1977, the Nobel Prize-winning economist Professor Milton Friedman placed the blame for Canada's growing economic difficulties on government deficits and excessive growth of the money supply. "There is only one place inflation is made in Canada and that is in Ottawa," he said bluntly. By 1981, conventional wisdom in much of the industrialized world blamed inflation on excessive growth in the money supply.

With consumer prices rising at more than 12% per year, the Bank of Canada followed the U.S. Federal Reserve and other central banks in boosting interest rates to record levels. In 1981, a business loan cost 19% a year and Canadian families were paying $1,500 per month for a home mortgage that would cost less than $650 at today's rates. The result was predictable. Companies stopped hiring, consumers stopped spending and the North American economy, as well as much of Europe's economy, contracted sharply. For Canada, it was the worst recession since the 1930s. In 1983, almost 1.5 million people were out of work: the unemployment rate was 11.9%.

Nor was the recovery from this recession typical. Even though the GDP grew for six consecutive years, there were still more than a million people out of work in 1989 and Canadian incomes had not improved since 1980. In the face of growing global market competition, large corporations had now begun to invest heavily in labour-saving technology. The era of restructuring and downsizing had begun, sweeping first through manufacturing and later through the service sector. As former finance minister Michael Wilson put it, Canada had acquired "an acute shortage of rich people."

GIVING CANADIANS "Amma (Icelandic for Grandmother) spent her last years, after the death of her husband, and after having had 12 children of her own, as a midwife. She would travel from home to home, attending to the birth and then would stay on to help with the household chores and the cooking for a few days until the new mother was on her feet. If her clients could pay her, fine. If not, there was never any question of a debt. Amma simply moved on to another neighbourhood assignment. That's the way it was during the Depression. People helped each other."

This anecdote tells of a part of life in Canada that is seldom considered and rarely applauded. Canadians are widely involved in our society; our charitable works form part of our national character and have since the earliest days of nationhood, when social services were provided not by the state but by religious groups, friends and family, and later charities.

The latest figures (for 1997) show that about 31% of adult Canadians are involved in some kind of volunteer work. This is up from 27% in 1987. With 7.5 million Canadians thus hard at work, our total volunteer hours in 1997 came to 1.11 billion.

(Below left)
Toronto, Ontario,
c. 1900-1910.
Photo by W. James,
courtesy National Archives
of Canada,
PA-118220.

(Below right)
Miss Brown, Toronto,
Ontario.
Photo by Pamela Harris.

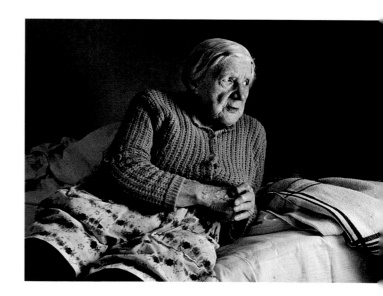

Nor is our concern for the well-being of others limited to giving only of our time. In 1997, some 88% of adults donated money to charitable organizations for a total of nearly $4.5 billion.

Generally, the more education one has, the more one is likely to give. Married Canadians have a greater likelihood of being charitable donors than are those who are single, separated, divorced or widowed. The likelihood of a financial donation also increases with age.

It is essential to note the important role of religion in giving. Canadians who belong to a faith, regardless of what it is, are far more likely to give than those without such a connection. Thus, while 73% of all Canadians had a religious affiliation, they accounted for fully 88% of all charitable donations in 1997.

What seems to be common to all Canadians who give of their time or money is altruism. As a people, we feel compassion for those in need and we want to help causes in which we believe. We also feel a sense of responsibility to our communities—a trait we've had, it would appear, since the creation of this country, since Amma's generation.

CANADIAN CREDIT There are more Visa and MasterCards in Canada than there are Canadians. In 1998, we numbered 30.3 million people against 35.3 million of these credit cards. Just 10 years earlier, as we numbered 25.3 million people, we owned about 19.4 million bank credit cards. We are not alone. In 1998, in the United States, with its population of about 270 million people, there were 300 million Visa and MasterCard accounts.

Canadian banks tell us that about half of credit-card holders pay off the balance owing on their cards each month. In the United States, only one-third do. In late 1997, Canadians owed a collective $23.9 billion on their bank credit cards while Americans owed $545 billion.

Such math presages bankruptcy. Not surprisingly, in 1997, some 85,000 Canadians, or 1 in 350, declared personal bankruptcy. In 1966, about 1 in 10,500 Canadians declared personal bankruptcy. In 1997, the personal bankruptcy rate hit a record high in the U.S. when 1.19 million Americans reported bankruptcy—or about 1 in 223.

Not all bank cards are used for credit. Banks and other financial institutions now issue a new type of card known as the debit or money card. These cards allow Canadians to access their accounts electronically. As of the end of 1998, there were some 23,500 "money" machines (also called automated banking machines) scattered across the Canadian landscape and more than 280,000 retail and other outlets where payments could be made using the card. In 1998, Canadians used these machines nearly 1.4 billion times.

WHEAT FROM THE CHAFF As far back as 1634 a Jesuit missionary wrote about the difficulty of growing wheat in Canada: "we sowed some in the autumn . . . in some places it was lost under the snow, in others it was so preserved that no finer wheat can be seen in France. We do not yet know very well which time is best . . . before winter to put in the seed."

Yet, from this tentative beginning, through a combination of chance and ingenuity, Canadians have become so accomplished at producing high-quality wheat that, by the early part of this century, Western Canada had earned the reputation of "the world's bread basket."

One marker of Canadian success in growing wheat was the development of Red Fife. In 1842, David Fife, a farmer in Upper Canada, planted wheat seeds from Poland that had been sent to him by a friend in Scotland. Not knowing that it was winter wheat, which requires a period of cold before it matures, he sowed the seeds as if they were spring wheat. Out of all the wheat planted, only one head of kernels grew, from spring wheat, accidentally mixed in with the rest. Fife saved the seed and planted it the following spring. It then grew so fast and proved so prolific that farmers as far away as the Red River settlement turned to this hardy new strain, which eventually became known as Red Fife.

Between 1892 and 1907, breeders crossed Red Fife with local Indian wheat. The result was the hardy Marquis wheat, which needed an even shorter growing season. By the early 1920s, Marquis had become so popular that it accounted for fully 90% of the spring wheat grown in Western Canada.

Le restaurant de Sam Latour.
Work by Miyuki Tanobe,
courtesy Musée du Québec.

Millennial Canada

The 1980s and 1990s marked a time of sweeping change in Canada's economic policies. The Canada–U.S. Free Trade Agreement (FTA), later expanded to Mexico under NAFTA, consigned the last vestiges of Macdonald's National Policy to the history books. Throughout the 1980s and 1990s, Crown corporations such as PetroCanada and Air Canada were sold to the private sector. The Foreign Investment Review Agency was replaced by a new agency called Investment Canada whose job was now to actively solicit foreign capital. Government regulations were also loosened to encourage competition in air transportation, trucking, telecommunications, broadcasting and other industries.

While governments in Canada and around the world experimented with new economic policies, in the early 1990s many central banks, including the Bank of Canada, applied traditional medicine to bring price inflation under control. In Canada, the policy was successful in lowering the annual rate of consumer price increases from 5% in 1989 to just 1.5% in 1992. However, business and consumer spending contracted as they had done a decade earlier. The economy scarcely grew at all in 1990 and, the following year, the GDP fell by almost 2%.

The recession of the early 1990s was not as severe as its 1980s counterpart, but it took longer for the economy to recover. Unemployment remained above 10% until 1995 and only toward the end of the decade did the economic picture really begin to brighten. Nearly 450,000 new jobs were created in 1998, the best annual performance of the decade.

One of the developments that pulled Canada out of this recession was the new boom in exports to the United States. In 1993, the economy grew by 2.5% and in 1994, by 3.9% on the strength of a 46% jump in exports to the American market. Expansion slowed through the middle years of the decade until the Bank of Canada, less concerned about inflation, loosened its monetary policy, and sent interest rates to record lows. In response, businesses and consumers borrowed heavily to purchase new machinery and equipment, homes, cars and appliances. This pushed the growth rate back up to 3.7% in 1997.

The upward trend continued into 1998 until an economic and financial crisis took hold in Japan, Korea, Thailand and other Asian countries. As a result, world demand for timber, minerals, energy and other raw materials —which make up around a quarter of Canada's exports—slumped badly. Canada's resource industries and farmers were hit hard by falling commodity prices. The economy grew by just 3% in 1998 and the Canadian dollar, which began the year worth more than 69 cents American, fell to an all-time low of less than 65 cents.

Jobs Through the 1990s, global economic forces combined with government policy to re-weave the fabric of Canada's labour market. "Downsizing," the term coined for shrinking corporations in the 1980s, spread to the public sector as governments cut programs and staff to balance budgets. Between 1990 and 1997, while overall employment grew by 775,000, the number of public sector jobs fell by some 88,000.

Willingly or otherwise, hundreds of thousands of Canadians left the traditional 9-to-5 job for early retirement, part-time work or to become their own bosses. Growth in self-employment, including home-based businesses, was explosive and accounted for 80% of the employment increase in Canada between 1989 and 1997.

The strongest job growth occurred in the service industry, which employs three working Canadians out of every four. The business services subsector grew faster than any other. In 1997, there were a million business service workers in the country, double the number in 1986. They included accountants, management consultants, maintenance people and more than 267,000 computer programmers and systems analysts, whose numbers grew by 92% in the five years following the recession.

Recent trends in the job market demonstrate that in a knowledge-based economy, employment opportunities, income and education are strongly correlated. The rapidly growing and increasingly well-paid business services sector, for example, employs more university graduates than any other sector except for health care. Since 1990, some 17% of jobs filled by people with less than a high school education have disappeared, while the number of jobs filled by people with postsecondary education have increased by nearly 30%.

Young People Since as early as 1946, the jobless rate for young people (15 to 24 years of age) has been about twice the average for the whole work force. In the 1990s, the rate of new job creation so trailed population growth that an expanded pool of adults was driven to compete for jobs in fast food, retail sales and other fields where young people have tended to work. Not surprisingly, the jobless rate for young people shot to nearly 18% during the recession of the early 1990s.

With such poor employment prospects, young people withdrew from the labour market in record numbers and many returned to school. In 1995, about 56% of young people in Canada were enrolled in some sort of postsecondary education compared with 40% in the late 1980s. Those who completed their studies had a much easier time finding work. They were one-third as likely to be unemployed as young people with less than high school education and their real wages were as much as 30% higher. In 1998, the unemployment rate for young people fell to under 14.5% as the economy created 143,000 jobs for youth, the best record in 20 years.

Income In 1941, female workers in Canada earned, on average, 32 cents an hour while males earned 54 cents. This wage gap scarcely budged for the next 25 years, until it began to close gradually during the 1970s. By 1997, Canadian women earned an average wage of $13.93 per hour—nearly 20% behind the average for men.

"One of the greatest pieces of economic wisdom is to know what you do not know."

John Kenneth Galbraith

In 1997, the average Canadian worker earned about $610 a week, including overtime. This was a $100-a-week improvement from the beginning of the decade, but this 15% increase was more than taken up by inflation. The average hourly wage for Canada's 3.6 million trade union members is about $19.00, compared with $15.64 an hour for non-union workers.

While wages and salaries account for three-quarters of the incomes of Canadians, there are other sources as well. Many Canadians receive money from government programs like Employment Insurance, Old Age Security and tax credits. In the 1970s, these transfers from government comprised about 10% of personal incomes in Canada. Now, with higher unemployment and an aging population, the figure is over 12%. Transfer programs are the backbone of our social safety net and help to even out the distribution of income in the country. Single-parent families headed by women receive almost a third of their income through transfer programs. For elderly couples, the figure is closer to 50%.

Since 1980, the gap in earnings between the richest and poorest segments of Canadian families has grown considerably. In 1996, the top 20% of Canadian families earned 22 times more than the poorest 20% of families. After taxes and transfers, however, the richest had incomes only five times more than the poorest and this ratio has remained very stable through the years.

Many Canadians also make some of their living from investments in stocks and bonds and interest on their bank accounts. Investments account for about 11% of the total personal income earned by all Canadians. In 1997, some 7.5 million Canadians had investment earnings totalling $26 billion.

Spending and Savings Although the sources of personal income have been stable for some time, Canadian spending patterns have changed dramatically. In 1961, we spent 85 cents of every dollar we earned on goods and services. About 28 cents went for housing and 16 cents for food. We paid 10 cents in taxes and put 3.5 cents into our bank accounts. In the late 1990s, a typical Canadian family spent 72 cents of each dollar earned on goods and services of which housing took 16 cents and food another 10 cents. About 25 cents went to taxes, while scarcely a penny went into personal savings.

Canadians used to be among the most diligent savers in the world. Through the 1980s, we put up to 15% of our annual incomes into savings accounts where they earned a good return. By the mid-1990s, Canadians were saving for their retirement mainly through pension plans and Registered Retirement Savings Plans. With interest rates falling, people virtually stopped saving. In fact, many people who had been savers have turned into borrowers in the last decade. In 1990, Canadians owed $366 billion in consumer loans and home mortgages. By 1998, Canadians had outstanding debts of $552 billion.

"Some people think Canada's vehicle is the train, or perhaps the snowmobile, but really it's the rowboat. We go forward, facing back."

John Gray, playwright and performer

Public Finances Like families and individuals, federal, provincial and local governments also receive revenues from various sources, such as personal and corporate income tax, property taxes, customs duties and user fees. In 1917, Canada's first income tax was implemented. Intended as a means of paying our military bills from the First World War, it was imposed by the federal government as a short-term measure. Total federal revenues from personal income taxes in the first year were $8 million. However, as C.D. Howe, the Minister of Trade and Commerce, would joke some 40 years later, "there is nothing more permanent than a temporary government building, unless it is a temporary tax." Some 80 years later, in 1998, the federal and provincial governments collected more than $130 billion in income taxes, which accounted for more than 31% of total government revenues.

Governments can also borrow money to finance long-term capital investments like roads and hospitals or to pay their bills when spending on programs exceeds their total revenues. For the federal, and many of the provincial governments, deficit spending became a standard practice from the 1970s until well into the 1990s. Between 1971 and 1998, for example, federal government debt grew from $18.6 billion to $584.4 billion, the equivalent initially of about $863 for each woman, man and child, to finally more than $19,000 per person. The bulk of this debt is owed to our own citizens and financial institutions who hold Canada Savings Bonds, treasury bills and other government securities. The remainder is owed to foreign lenders. William Lyon Mackenzie King, who was Canada's longest serving prime minister, once exclaimed, "the promises of yesterday are the taxes of today." In the late 1980s and through much of the 1990s, federal and provincial governments raised tax rates to meet current obligations and to pay the interest on funds they had borrowed in the past. During this period, governments began to trim expenditures on many programs. Total spending by the federal and provincial governments peaked in 1995 and declined through the latter years of the decade.

The combination of rising tax receipts and reduced spending has led to a dramatic change in Canada's public finances. In the 1997–98 fiscal year, the federal government recorded its first budget surplus in 28 years, and by early in the new millennium, all provinces are expected to be in similar positions.

Cypress River, Manitoba.

Photo by Mike Grandmaison.

JAZZ, IN ITS TRUE STATE, IS A SPONTANEOUS, ADVENTUROUS AND EMOTIONAL

REACTION. JAZZ MUSICIANS MUST LEARN TO REACT QUICKLY TO CHANGING HARMONIES

AS THEY FLY BY THEM IN THEIR SOLOS. EVEN AS THEY IMPROVISE, THEY MUST STILL,

IN MANY CASES, PLAY OVER BARS OF FOUR BEATS AND SOMETIMES OVER THREE-

QUARTER WALTZ TIME OR "FIVE-FOUR" OR "SIX-EIGHT" TIME. IT HAS ALWAYS BEEN

MY CONTENTION THAT JAZZ MUSICIANS, PRIMARILY BECAUSE OF THIS MIX OF SPONTA-

NEITY AND DISCIPLINE, ARE PERHAPS THE GREATEST MATHEMATICIANS IN THE WORLD.

Oscar Peterson, musician

(Opposite page) Detail from Canadiana Suite, last four measures of "Place St. Henri."

Canadian men's relay team
wins gold at the Atlanta
Olympics, 1996.
(Left to right) Bruny Surin,
Glenroy Gilbert, Donovan
Bailey, Robert Esmie.
Photo by Claus Andersen,
Canadian Sport Images.

CANADA IN THE WORLD

In 1938, Dr. Norman Bethune, a surgeon from Gravenhurst, Ontario, journeyed to China to bring medical care to Mao Tse-tung's Communist armies and is beloved in that country to this day.

In 1949, the pianist Oscar Peterson performed at Carnegie Hall, becoming the first Canadian to have a major international impact on jazz. His *Canadiana Suite* has been called a landscape in sound reminiscent of the art of A.Y. Jackson.

Glenn Gould's recordings of a Bach prelude and fugue were among the artifacts on two *Voyager* spacecraft launched by NASA in the 1970s. Jean Vanier, born to a prosperous family and the son of a Governor General, founded L'Arche, an international network of communities that welcome people with developmental handicaps.

Vanier, Gould and Peterson join countless other Canadians who have defied Canadian borders, extending them to include the entire world through artistic or humanitarian or medical pursuits. Their myriad contributions have touched the lives of countless people throughout the world.

The work of Dr. Frederick Banting and Charles Best, who discovered insulin at the University of Toronto in the 1920s, has saved the lives of millions of diabetics. Since its publication in 1908, Lucy Maud Montgomery's story of a red-haired orphan, *Anne of Green Gables*, has charmed readers worldwide and drawn millions to visit Prince Edward Island, the setting for this novel.

Canadians also seem to have a national talent for inventions, and for engineering feats, surely inspired by the challenges posed by time and space in a country this size. The snowmobile and standard time are two such Canadian inventions, as is the robotic arm used on space shuttles.

To bridge the sheer size of Canada's space, we have engineered some of the contemporary wonders of the world. The Trans-Canada highway, which spans 7,821 km, is the longest national highway in the world. Yonge Street, stretching more than 1,900 km from Toronto to the Ontario–Minnesota border, is the longest designated street in the world. Confederation Bridge, which at 12.9 km connects Prince Edward Island to Canada's mainland, is the world's longest bridge over ice-covered waters. The West Edmonton Mall, which spans an area equal to 48 city blocks, is the world's largest indoor mall.

We have also created some much beloved forms of fun enjoyed the planet over: hockey, basketball, ginger ale and even good children's reading. The early books of the Hardy Boys detective series were written by none other than Canadian-born Leslie McFarlane, under the pen name of Franklin W. Dixon, and have sold more than 50 million books around the world.

World Records

Since 1992, the United Nations has ranked Canada six times as the best place in the world to live. Such an encomium is unsurpassed by any other country in the world. In granting it, the United Nations looks at a wide variety of economic and social areas such as life expectancy, health conditions, education and incomes.

Incomes For instance, in 1995, Canadians had an average per capita income of

"Diabetus. Ligate pancreatic ducts of dog. Keep dogs alive till acini degenerate leaving Islets. Try to isolate the internal secretion of these to relieve glycosuria."

Frederick Banting, notes scribbled October 31, 1920, which led to the discovery of insulin

$22,000 (measured by purchasing power parity or PPPs which are the indices used to compare the prices of the same basket of goods and services in different countries). At the same time, citizens of other industrialized countries had average incomes of $16,000 compared with $6,000 for all world citizens. Canadian incomes were similar to those in Norway, Denmark and Japan, while Luxembourg ($34,000), Brunei Darussalam ($31,000) and the United States ($27,000) had, on average, higher per capita incomes than Canada.

Although the gap between the rich and poor widened during the 1990s, this difference has traditionally been less extreme in Canada than in many other nations. Between 1980 and 1994, again using PPPs, the poorest 20% of Canadians had an average per capita income of $5,971 while the richest 20% had an average income of $42,110. In the United States, for example, the gap was slightly larger. The average income was $5,800 for the poorest 20% of the population and $51,705 for the richest 20%.

Health In terms of life expectancy, a baby born in Canada today can look forward to living 79.1 years. Only people in Japan (79.9 years) and Iceland (79.2 years) can expect to live longer. Life expectancy in the United States is 76.4 years and the world average is 63.6 years.

Between 1986 and 1996, spending on health in Canada rose from 8.7% to 9.6% of GDP, making Canada the fifth largest spender in the world after the United States (14.0%), Germany (10.5%), France (9.7%) and Switzerland (9.7%).

In Canada, because both rich and poor have access to health care, our infant mortality rate has traditionally been lower than the average rate in many industrialized countries. In 1995, according to the Organisation for Economic Co-operation and Development (OECD), Canada's infant mortality rate stood at 6 deaths per 1,000 live births, compared with 8 deaths per 1,000 live births in the United States.

Our maternal mortality rate, which refers to the number of women that die during childbirth, has dropped from 500 deaths per 100,000 live births in the early 1920s to less than 5 per 100,000 in the 1990s, among the lowest in the world. An African woman's lifetime risk of dying from pregnancy-related causes is estimated to be 1 in 23; for a Canadian woman it is less than 1 in 4,000.

Education Canada spends more generously on education than do most other countries, including the United States. In 1995, Canada devoted some 7.6% of GDP to education while the U.S. spent 6.7%. In Canada, like most industrialized nations, the majority of people can read and write, although literacy skills can vary considerably.

In 1995, the United Nations found that almost 17% of Canadians were considered functionally illiterate, which means their skills were too limited to allow them to deal with most of the written material used in everyday life. The rate was higher in the United Kingdom at 21.8%, and in the United States at 20.7%. The lowest rates in the world were in Sweden, where an estimated 7.5% of the population was considered functionally illiterate, and in the Netherlands, where the rate was only 10.8%.

Despite a United Nations pledge to make education as accessible to girls as to boys, there are still great disparities throughout much of the world. Interestingly, however, in Canada, women now account for the majority of students in university. This was one of the reasons that, in 1998, Canada ranked first in the United Nations' index of women's development, followed by Norway, Sweden, Iceland, Finland, the United States and France. In that same year, women held 21% of parliamentary seats in Canada, compared with an average of 15% for industrialized countries and 12% for all nations.

Research and Development Since the days of the first long-distance telephone call between Brantford and Paris, Ontario, Canada has led in the use of technology that takes the bite out of distance. With the advent of a global economy, there has been an increasing pressure to maintain our technological prowess. In 1996, Canada invested just 1.6% of GDP in research and development—well below the 2.2% average for all OECD countries. Japan (2.8%) and the United States (2.6%) invested more heavily.

Nevertheless, Canada has a strong presence in cyberspace and is a world leader in the rapidly changing field of electronic commerce. In 1995, Canadians banked electronically an average of 46 times compared with 37 times for Americans and 25 times for people in the United Kingdom. In the most recently available survey of all industrialized powers, Canada had the lowest Internet charges in 1996. The average price among developed countries was $81.54 for 20 hours. The average Canadian spent just $28.36 for 20 hours.

A Trading Nation

Canada has always been a trading nation. As early as 1926, we exported 30% of our total production to other countries. In the 1990s, trade assumed an even greater importance. In 1997, over 40% of our GDP was generated by exports—more than the United States (12%) and more than all other G7 countries (18%). Today, Industry Canada estimates that one in three Canadian jobs depends on trade.

Overall, we are selling and buying more than ever before. As the 1990s draw to a close, our balance of payments—the measure that totals all the transactions between Canada and the world—has reached record highs.

In 1998, Canada sold $402.5 billion in goods and services to other countries, a dramatic increase from 1993 when we sold a total of $235.5 billion. In the same year, we bought a total of $420.9 billion in goods and services from other countries, another strong increase from a total of $263.7 billion in 1993. In 1998, our sales abroad grew more than our purchases from foreign markets, which reduced our net purchases from other countries to $18.4 billion, down from $28.1 billion in 1993.

In 1996, by UN measure, four Canadian companies were among the top 100 transnational companies: publishing conglomerate Thomson Corp., beverage-maker Seagram Corp. and telecommunications giants BCE Inc. and Northern Telecom (Nortel). Seagram was rated the most transnational company in the world that year.

(Left)

Cour d'école, 1941. Work by Jean-Charles Faucher, courtesy Musée du Québec.

One of the factors that has contributed to the growth of trade has been a low Canadian dollar. In the past 25 years, Canadians have watched as its value dropped in comparison with the American dollar. In 1974, it took 99 cents to buy one U.S. dollar; by 1998, it took $1.48. A lower Canadian dollar has increased the cost of imports and forced Canadians to pay more to travel abroad. On the other hand, it has also meant that Canada's goods and services are less expensive to the rest of the world.

What We Trade Historically, Canada has been known to the rest of the world as a rich source of raw materials and primary products, including lumber, minerals, oil and wheat. Canada is, in fact, the world's largest exporter of forestry products, with more than 16% of total world exports. Over the past 25 years, however, the source of our exports has shifted. Resources now represent only about 20% of Canada's total exports, compared with 40% in 1963.

The shift began after the Second World War as Canadian workers began migrating from farms to factories. The 1965 Auto Pact with the United States was a pivotal agreement; it strengthened an automobile industry that has been a major engine of prosperity in Canada since the 1960s. In 1998, more than half a million people worked in the automobile industry, and today, Canada ranks sixth in world automotive production.

Arguably, a second shift began in the 1970s, as the balance of economic activity swung from manufacturing to services. In Canada, services now represent 75% of our GDP. Between 1988 and 1997, our exports of services more than doubled from $19 billion to $42 billion.

Traditionally, Canadians have imported more services from other countries than we've sold in international markets. However, in the 1990s, the growth in the export of services accelerated and the deficit on all services dropped from $13.6 billion to $8.7 billion between 1993 and 1997.

Where We Trade During much of Canada's history, reciprocity or free trade with the United States has been a major issue. In 1911, the Conservative Party won an election under the slogan "No truck nor trade with the Yankees." Even earlier, in the 1830s, Thomas Haliburton created Sam Slick, a popular fictional character who made a mockery of American imports.

Today, the Canada–U.S. trade relationship is the most significant trade partnership in the world, accounting for more than $1 billion per day in two-way trade. Although Canada sells goods and services around the world, more than 80% of our exports and close to 70% of our imports are with the United States.

Together, the Canada–U.S. Free Trade Agreement in 1988 and the North American Free Trade Agreement (NAFTA) in 1994 liberalized trading relationships with our southern neighbour and with Mexico. With free trade, we've become even more dependent on our exports to the United States.

"Foreign policy is merely domestic policy with its hat on."

Lester B. Pearson

Much of this trade involves affiliates of international corporations, a sign of the seamless relationship that can exist between major trading partners. In 1995, some 54.5% of exports from Canada to the U.S. originated with foreign-controlled firms and 63.4% of imports to Canada from the U.S. were by foreign-controlled firms.

By region, the European Union (EU) consistently comes in second as our most important trading partner. The EU market has also experienced the fastest growth in trade with Canada of any non-U.S. market. Between 1985 and 1996, our exports to the EU grew by nearly 37% while exports to Japan increased by 21%.

Foreign Investment

While Canada has been trading more than ever before, we have also been investing outside our country at record levels. Our overall level of foreign direct investment is considerably higher than that of other G7 countries. In 1996, Canadians invested the equivalent of a total of 22% of GDP in other countries, compared with 12% for all G7 nations. Foreign direct investment coming into Canada totalled 21% of GDP compared with 8% for all G7 countries.

Historically, Canada has had more direct investment come into the country from foreign sources than we have invested in other countries. In recent years, that pattern has changed dramatically. For instance, in 1960, some $13.6 billion came into Canada in foreign direct investment while Canadians invested $2.6 billion in other countries. By 1996, Canadians actually had more invested outside Canada than other countries had invested inside Canada. That year, Canadians invested $177 billion around the world while other countries invested $174.6 billion in Canada.

In 1997, the scales continued to tip slightly in Canada's favour. Canadian direct investment overseas grew by 9% to $194 billion while investment from other countries in Canada rose 7% to $188 billion. The trend persisted in 1998 with Canadian firms increasing their direct investment abroad by 17% to $240 billion and foreigners increasing their direct investment in Canada by 10% to $217 billion.

As well as being our major trading partner, the United States is our leading source of direct foreign investment. In 1997, the U.S. was responsible for 70% of foreign investment into Canada. Other key investors were the United Kingdom (8%), other members of the European Union (12%), Japan and other OECD countries (7%) and all other countries (3%).

In 1997, Canadian investment outside our country showed a more diverse pattern. Slightly more than half, or 52%, of Canadian investment went to the United States. Other investment destinations were the United Kingdom (10%), other members of the European Union (11%), Japan and other OECD countries (5%) and all other countries (22%).

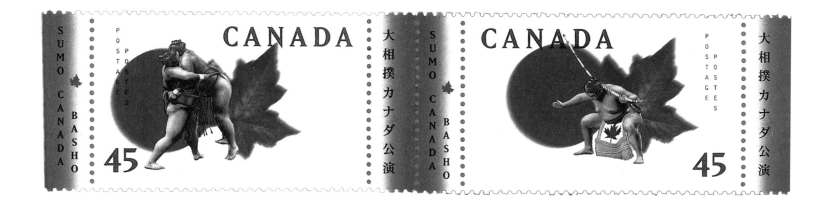

Sumo Canada Basho, 1998.
Courtesy Canada Post
Corporation.

Canada in the World

As a trading nation, Canada must rely on strong international relationships. In 1998, the Department of Foreign Affairs and International Trade had more than 250 missions around the world in major cities ranging from Abidjan to Zagreb. Canada maintains membership in a host of international organizations from the World Bank to the International Center for Genetic Engineering and Biotechnology.

As an officially bilingual nation, Canada is one of a handful of countries in the world that are members of both the Commonwealth, the association of former British colonies, and La Francophonie, an alliance of French-speaking countries.

Canada helped found the Organisation for Economic Co-operation and Development in 1961. Over the years, the OECD has grown to 29 members, including 22 European nations, the three North American countries, and four Asian nations. Based in Paris, France, the OECD gathers and analyses statistics that help governments plan their economic policies.

More recently, Canada also supported the development of the World Trade Organization (WTO), founded in 1995, which replaced the General Agreement on Tariffs and Trade (GATT).

The WTO is the largest and most comprehensive trade-negotiation organization ever formed. Its purpose is to free up trade among the world's nations by streamlining customs duties, negotiating trade agreements and settling trade disputes. The WTO not only took over the old GATT, which dealt with trade in goods, but also took on new agreements on services, investment and intellectual property.

Since 1976, Canada has been a member of the Group of Seven, or G7 as it's called (the club expanded to the G8 in 1998 when Russia was welcomed as a full partner), and has met annually with the world's major industrialized democracies (France, Germany, Italy, Japan, Britain and the United States) to deal with pressing global economic and political issues. This exclusive club has come to act as the world's *de facto* inner cabinet, and has been focusing of late on the challenges posed by the rapid pace of globalization.

THE BUG THAT ROARED It may well be the "bug that roared." In its simplest terms, Y2K refers to a computer glitch that could mean that some computers and computer programs will confuse the date change coming on January 1, 2000.

The problem begins with a tiny crystal of silicon called a microchip—about the width of a human hair and etched with electrical pathways—which drives almost everything in our daily lives, from water purification systems to phone systems and from elevators to trains. Since few microchips are programmed to recognize the year 2000, when the clock strikes midnight on December 31, 1999, this ubiquitous silicon crystal could well default on its responsibilities.

Nor does the problem stop here. While the microchip powers the computer, there are also the computer programs themselves that are equally powerful in running many of the critical systems of modern society, such as banking systems and elevators. Like the microchip, many of these programs were also created using

2 0

only two digits to indicate the date, so as they come upon the year 2000, they will simply read 1900 or 00 and thus may be disabled or generate faulty results.

As the millennium nears, Canadian industries and governments have been spending literally billions of dollars to ensure that everything running on a microchip, or a computer program, continues at the start of the year 2000. Y2K programmers are in such high demand that they have been commanding annual salaries of up to $100,000 or more.

When Canadian thinker Marshall McLuhan first coined the phrase "the global village" in 1967, he may not have realized how profoundly something like the Y2K bug could affect the world. Computers have so drawn the planet together that Y2K is not simply a Canadian problem; it's planetary and it's been estimated that the global cost of reparation could go as high as US$1 trillion.

In Canada, police forces and military troops will be on standby in the last few days of 1999—not for combat purposes, but as a measure of precaution against the Y2K bug.

TIME OF A MILLENNIUM What's in a millennium? In the one coming up, it's easy enough to count: 10 centuries, 100 decades, and 1,000 years. But then it gets tricky. Best records show 242 leap years and 12,000 months, or 365,242 days, or 8,765,808 hours, or 525,948,480 minutes or 31,556,908,800 seconds! This doesn't count the extra seconds that must be added to account for the slowing of the Earth's rotation. By the end of the third millennium (the year 3000), these should total about half an hour.

Chronicling the total moments in a millennium begs the issue of time. If you trace time to its origins in Canada, it would appear it began in 1582. That was the year the Gregorian calendar came into use in New France (the 17th-century Maritimes and southern Quebec). In 1752, the rest of what is now Canada adopted the Gregorian calendar. The work of Pope Gregory XIII, this calendar compensated for the six extra hours of each year in the Julian calendar by adding leap years.

At the end of the first millennium, a point when many believed the world would end, a monk, writer and prophet named Raoul Glaber wrote, "We see clearer than daylight that in process of the Last Days, as love [has] waxed cold and iniquity [has] abounded among mankind, perilous times [are] at hand for men's souls."

Since then, another thousand years have come and gone.

CANADIAN DREAMERS Canada's first patent was granted in 1791 to Angus MacDonnel, a Scottish soldier garrisoned at Québec, and Samuel Hopkins of Vermont, for processing potash and soap from wood ash.

In 1890, a Calgary woman invented a mechanical skirt lifter to allow her to raise her hem discreetly before crossing a muddy or dusty street.

During the Second World War, Dr. Wilbur Franks of Toronto invented the anti-gravity flying suit, which allowed a pilot wearing it to withstand pressure equal to eight times the force of gravity.

Canada has always, it would appear, had a gold mine of dreamers and risk-takers who have invented wild and wonderful things. Some of these inventions have everyday uses—for example, the paint roller, first created by Norman Breakey, and the zipper, the brainchild of Gideon Sundback.

Other Canadian inventions have altered the destiny of the world. Aeronautical engineer Wallace Rupert Turnbull's 1916 variable-pitch propeller—a device which adjusts the angle of flying airplanes—was a major leap forward in aviation safety. Joseph-Armand Bombardier invented the snowmobile in 1959. In 1981, Canadarm, the National Research Council's satellite launcher, took its maiden flight.

Today, inventions are primarily the result of cumulative small-scale improvements and are more likely to be made through government- or industry-sponsored research, thus making it difficult to keep an accurate count of the number of Canadian inventions. But we do know that more than 1.3 million patents have been issued in Canada since 1824.

(Right)

Dr. Gerhard Herzberg.

Work by D.C. Lewis.

(Far right)

Dr. Frederick Banting,

Toronto, Ontario,

c. 1920–1925.

Photo by Arthur S. Goss,

courtesy National Archives

of Canada, PA-123481.

(Opposite page)

Dr. Charles Best.

Courtesy National Archives

of Canada, C-037763,

Royal Society of Canada

Collection.

CANADA'S NOBELS The first Nobel Prizes were handed out in 1901. The Swedish industrialist, Alfred Nobel, requested that a fund be established for prizes in his name for outstanding achievement in physics, chemistry, physiology or medicine, literature and peace. In 1969, a Nobel Prize for economics was introduced, endowed by the Bank of Sweden.

Since then, 16 Canadians have been awarded a Nobel in five of the six categories: **Frederick Banting** and **John Macleod**, physiology and medicine, 1923; **William Giaque**, chemistry, 1949; Prime Minister **Lester Pearson**, peace, 1957; **Gerhard Herzberg**, chemistry, 1971; **David Hubel**, medicine, 1981; **Arthur Schalow**, physics, 1981; **Henry Taube**, chemistry, 1983; **John Polanyi**, chemistry, 1986; **Sidney Altman**, chemistry, 1989; **Richard Taylor**, physics, 1990; **Rudolf Marcus**, chemistry, 1992; **Michael Smith**, physics, 1993; **Bertram Brockhouse**, physics, 1994; **William Vickrey**, economics, 1996; **Myron Scholes**, economics, 1997.

Many other laureates have had links to Canada. Guglielmo Marconi won the Nobel Prize for physics in 1909. Eight years earlier, he had received the world's first transatlantic radio transmission in St. John's, Newfoundland, wired in Morse code from Cornwall, England. Ernest Hemingway, who won the Nobel Prize for literature in 1954, once wrote articles for the *Toronto Star* and *Star Weekly*, and William Faulkner, who won the literature prize in 1949, was, for a short while, a member of the Royal Canadian Air Force.

Clay formations, near Marble
Canyon, British Columbia.
Photo by Mike Grandmaison.

The Environment

As custodian of 7% of the world's land mass, 9% of the earth's fresh water, and 24% of its wetlands, Canada has an inherent interest in the environment. Yet, in 1996, only about 9% of Canada was considered a protected area—a lower percentage than in the United States (19%), Denmark (32%) or New Zealand (23%).

In 1987, we joined in signing the Montréal Protocol, an agreement to reduce global levels of chlorofluorocarbons (CFCs) and a milestone in addressing the issue of global warming. In 1998, Canada signed the Kyoto Protocol, a commitment by industrialized countries to reduce their collective emissions of greenhouse gases by 5.2% before 2012.

During the 1980s, the term sustainable development entered the Canadian vocabulary. In 1983, the World Commission on Environment and Development defined this term as "development that meets the needs of the present without compromising the ability of future generations to meet their own needs."

Canada has been a leader in establishing standards to measure sustainable development. In addition, many businesses now recognize that cleaning up the environment offers good business opportunities. Today, about 4,500 Canadian companies are involved in environmental technology—one of our fastest growing industries, both in domestic and international markets.

Yet only two countries produce more garbage than Canada. In 1995, each person in the United States generated 730 kg of municipal waste. In Australia, the total was 690 kg. In Canada, the total was 670 kg. On the other hand, European countries generated only 414 kg per person.

The United Nations has estimated that a child born in the industrialized world adds more to the consumption of the planet's resources and pollution than 30 to 50 children born in less developed nations. The fifth of the world's population living in the highest-income countries are responsible for more than 50% of the world's emissions of carbon monoxide.

Tourism

Today, visitors come to Canada to enjoy our theatres and cultural events, as well as to paddle our lakes or to whale-watch off our ocean shores. Canada is one of the top 10 tourist destinations in the world. Tourism has been helped by the relatively low value of the Canadian dollar, travel by the wealthier baby boomers, growing disposable incomes in developing regions, and continuing visits by Americans.

In 1997, however, after 10 years of growth, international tourist travel activity fell and Canada was clearly affected by the trend. There were 3% fewer overnight trips by overseas visitors in 1997 than in the previous year. Also, the number of overnight Asian visitors dropped by 9% that year. However, more visitors from the United States helped to offset the decline in overseas travellers. Americans made 14.9 million overnight trips to Canada in 1998, up 11% from 1997. At the same time, Canadians reduced their number of trips to the United States to 13.4 million, the lowest annual level since 1987.

Almost every year since 1951, Canada has had a travel deficit. That is, Canadians have spent more outside the country than people from outside the country spend in Canada. Since 1980, Canada's travel receipts grew from $3 billion to more than $12 billion in 1997, and travel payments went from almost $4 billion to about $16 billion. In 1997, the deficit was $3.5 billion, an improvement from the $6.4 billion deficit in 1992.

Defence

In 1928, a Memorial Chamber was opened in the Peace Tower of Canada's Parliament Buildings. The chamber now houses six Books of Remembrance that honour the 114,710 sailors, soldiers, airmen, nurses, servicewomen and merchant marines who lost their lives while serving this country. The ceiling, walls and columns of the chamber are constructed of Château Gaillard stone, presented to Canada by France. The altar, a gift from Britain, rests on stone quarried from the fields of Flanders in Belgium.

Engraved on the wall is the poem "In Flanders Fields," written by Canadian surgeon John McCrae, which remembers the 66,655 Canadian soldiers who died during the First World War. When Canada signed the Treaty of Versailles in 1919 and joined the League of Nations as a country separate from Britain, many historians saw this as the true beginning of our nation-hood.

Canada has been called a "nation forged in fire" because of the important part that two world wars played in shaping Canada into a country. Today, we are not known as a military power. In 1996, we spent 1.5% of GDP on defence compared with 3.6% spent in the United States and 3.0% in the United Kingdom.

Yet, for a generation of Canadians, the Second World War left permanent emotional and physical scars. One million Canadians fought in this war; 44,893 died. There are also good memories: the Netherlands and Canada forged a friendship when Canada gave refuge to the Dutch royal family during the war. Canadian troops also fought in the liberation of Holland. Each year since 1945, thousands of Dutch tulips arrive for Ottawa's tulip festival as a sign of our lasting friendship.

Canadians also served with distinction in the Korean War. Approximately 27,000 Canadians served in Korea and more than 500 died. Canadian action in Korea was followed by other peacekeeping missions with Canadian troops deployed around the world.

Lester Pearson, Canada's 14th prime minister, began a legacy of Canadian involvement in peacekeeping during the Suez crisis in 1957 when he suggested that military personnel be used for non-violent roles, such as monitoring cease-fires. For this innovation, he was awarded the Nobel Peace Prize. Since then, Canada has joined virtually every major peacekeeping mission and humanitarian effort undertaken by the United Nations.

"In Flanders Fields the poppies blow

Between the crosses, row on row,

That mark our place; and in the sky

The larks, still bravely singing, fly

Scarce heard amid the guns below."

John McCrae, "In Flanders Fields"

Canadians have served in Cyprus, the former Yugoslavia, Haiti, Somalia, the Middle East and in many other parts of the world. More than 100 Canadian soldiers have been killed during nearly 50 years of peacekeeping missions.

Canada has sought peace in other ways. We helped establish the United Nations and currently have a seat on the UN Security Council. In 1986, Canada received a Nansen Medal for humanitarianism, presented for our assistance to refugees. It was the first and only time that an entire population has been given this award.

Under the leadership of Foreign Affairs Minister Lloyd Axworthy, Canada has also played a key role in controlling the use of land mines. In 1997, the Anti-Personnel Mine Ban Convention was signed by 122 countries in Ottawa. The treaty sets new international norms against mines. Canada set up a five-year $100-million fund to remove mines, assist victims, develop technology and help countries comply with the treaty. In 1998, Canadians helped form the International Criminal Court, an international tribunal empowered to prosecute individuals accused of genocide, war crimes, crimes against humanity and, in the future, crimes of aggression.

Foreign Aid

Although Canadian businesses are investing around the world more than ever before, the number of Canadian dollars directed to foreign aid and development has fallen. In 1996, Canada's official development assistance was equal to 0.32% of GDP, a drop from the 1986 rate of 0.49%. That came to about US$64 donated for every Canadian citizen, compared with $85 some 10 years earlier. Many other countries have also curtailed their rate of spending on foreign aid. Scandinavian countries, however, give far more generously. Between 1986 and 1996, their donations rose from $202 to $218 per capita.

The nature of aid has changed as well. Since a review in 1995, it has been Canada's policy to devote one-quarter of program dollars to basic human needs such as primary health care, basic education, family planning, nutrition, water and sanitation, as well as to providing humanitarian assistance in emergencies.

Canada has also linked its support of development projects to human rights obligations, the full participation of women as equal partners in the sustainable development of their societies, and the protection of the environment.

Detail of *Airplane Series*,
1985–86.
Work by Wanda Koop.
Photo by William Eakin.

Fort Amherst Lighthouse,
Newfoundland.
Photo by Norman Piluke,
Tony Stone.

BIBLIOGRAPHY: SELECTED SOURCES

The Land

Statistics Canada:
Human Activity and the Environment, 1994,
  Cat. No.11-509-XPE
Canadian Agriculture at a Glance, 1994,
  Cat. No. 96-301-XPB

Colombo, John Robert. *The 1999 Canadian
  Global Almanac*. Toronto: Macmillan, 1998.
Warkentin, John. *Canada: A Regional
  Geography*. Scarborough, Ont.: Prentice Hall,
  1997.

The People

Statistics Canada:
Canadian Social Trends, Cat. No. 11-008-XPE
*Language, Tradition, Health, Lifestyle, and
  Social Issues*, Cat. No. 89-533-XPB
Marriage and Conjugal Life in Canada,
  Cat. No. 91-534-XPE
Family Over the Life Course,
  Cat. No. 91-543-XPE
Knowledge of Languages—The Nation,
  Cat. No. 93-318-XPB
Religions in Canada, Cat. No. 93-319-XPB
Age and Sex, Cat. No. 94-327-XPB

The Society

Statistics Canada:
Education Quarterly Review,
  Cat. No. 81-003-XPB
Education in Canada, Cat. No. 81-229-XPB
Health Reports, Cat. No. 82-003-XPB
*National Population Health Survey Overview
  1996–97*, Cat. No. 82-567-XPB
Police Personnel and Expenditures in Canada,
  Cat. No. 85F00019-XPE
Juristat, Cat. No. 85-002-XPE
A Profile of Youth Justice in Canada,
  Cat. No. 85-544-XIE

National Forum on Health. *Canada Health
  Action: Building on the Legacy*. Ottawa,
  1997.

Arts and Leisure

Statistics Canada:
Services Indicators, Cat. No. 63-016-XPB
Sound Recording, Cat. No. 87F0008-XPE
Focus on Culture, Cat. No. 87-004-XPB
Performing Arts Survey, Cat. No. 87-209-XPB
*Canada's Culture, Heritage and Identity: A
  Statistical Perspective*, Cat. No. 87-211-XPB

BIBLIOGRAPHY: SELECTED SOURCES

The Economy

Statistics Canada:
Canadian Economic Observer,
    Cat. No. 11-010S-XPB
Income Distributions by Size in Canada,
    Cat. No. 13-207-XPB
Family Incomes, Cat. No. 13-208-XPB
Gross National Product by Industry,
    Cat. No. 15-512-XPB
The Consumer Price Index,
    Cat. No. 62-001-XPB
Labour Force Update, Cat. No. 71-005-XPB
Perspectives on Labour and Income,
    Cat. No. 75-011-XPE

Canada in the World

Statistics Canada:
Canada's Balance of International Payments,
    Cat. No. 67-001-XPB
Canada's International Investment Position,
    1997, Cat. No. 67-202-XPB
Travel-log, Cat. No. 87-003-XPB

Industry Canada. *Canada's Service Economy.*
    Ottawa, 1996.

Common Sources

Statistics Canada:
The Daily, Cat. No. 11-001E
Canada Year Book 1999, Cat. No. 11-402-XPE
Canada: A Portrait, 55th Edition,
    Cat. No. 11-403-XPE
Historical Statistics of Canada, 2nd edition,
    Cat. No. CS11-516E
1999 Canada at a Glance,
    Cat. No. 12-581-XPE
1996 Census Dictionary, Cat. No. 92-351-XPE

Gentilcore, L. and G.J. Matthews (eds.), 1993.
    Historical Atlas of Canada. Toronto:
    University of Toronto Press, 1987, 1990,
    1993.
*The 1999 Canadian Encyclopedia: World
    Edition*, CD-ROM. Toronto: McClelland &
    Stewart, 1998.

REGIONAL REFERENCE CENTRES

Statistics Canada national enquiries line:
1 800 263-1136

Toll-free order line (Canada and U.S.):
1 800 267-6677

National toll-free fax order line: 1 877 287-4369

National telecommunications device for the
hearing impaired line: 1 800 363-7629

Internet site: www.statcan.ca

Atlantic Region

Serving Newfoundland and Labrador,
Nova Scotia, Prince Edward Island and
New Brunswick.

Advisory Services
1741 Brunswick Street
2nd floor, Box 11
Halifax, Nova Scotia
B3J 3X8

Phone: (902) 426-5331
Fax: (902) 426-9538
E-mail: atlantic.info@statcan.ca

Quebec Region

Serving Quebec and the Territory of Nunavut.

Advisory Services
200 René Lévesque Blvd. West
Guy Favreau Complex
4th Floor, East Tower
Montréal, Quebec
H2Z 1X4

Phone: (514) 283-5725
Fax: (514) 283-9350

National Capital Region

Statistical Reference Centre
R.H. Coats Building Lobby
Holland Avenue
Ottawa, Ontario
K1A 0T6

Phone: (613) 951-8116
Fax: (613) 951-0581
E-mail: infostats@statcan.ca

Ontario Region

Advisory Services
Arthur Meighen Building, 10th Floor
25 St. Clair Avenue East
Toronto, Ontario
M4T 1M4

Phone: (416) 973-6586
Fax: (416) 973-7475

Prairie Region

Manitoba

Advisory Services
VIA Rail Building, Suite 200
123 Main Street
Winnipeg, Manitoba
R3C 4V9

Phone: (204) 983-4020
Fax: (204) 983-7543
E-mail: statswpg@solutions.net

REGIONAL REFERENCE CENTRES

Saskatchewan

Advisory Services
Park Plaza, Suite 440
2365 Albert Street
Regina, Saskatchewan
S4P 4K1

Phone: (306) 780-5405
Fax: (306) 780-5403
E-mail: statcan@sk.sympatico.ca

Southern Alberta

Advisory Services
Discovery Place, Room 201
3553–31 Street N.W.
Calgary, Alberta
T2L 2K7

Phone: (403) 292-6717
Fax: (403) 292-4958
E-mail: degagnej@cadvision.com

Northern Alberta and Northwest Territories

Advisory Services
Park Square, 9th Floor
10001 Belamy Hill
Edmonton, Alberta
T5J 3B6

Phone: (780) 495-3027
Fax: (780) 495-5318
E-mail: ewieall@statcan.ca

Pacific Region

Serving British Columbia and the Yukon Territory.

Advisory Services
Library Square Office Tower
600–300 West Georgia Street
Vancouver, British Columbia
V6B 6C7

Phone: (604) 666-3691
Fax: (604) 666-4863
E-mail: stcvan@statcan.ca

INDEX

Note: All references to Canada unless otherwise stated; "(i)" indicates a photograph or illustration.

CANADA

Scale: 1: 20 000 000

1 cm = 200 km

⊛ Federal capital

★ Provincial capital

● Other populated places

— · — · — · — · — International boundary

— ·· — ·· — ·· — ·· Provincial and territorial boundary

————🍁———— Trans-Canada Highway

Produced by Geography Division,

Statistics Canada